Accountability in
Health Facilities

Harry I. Greenfield
epilogue by
Amitai Etzioni

The Praeger Special Studies program—utilizing the most modern and efficient book production techniques and a selective worldwide distribution network—makes available to the academic, government, and business communities significant, timely research in U.S. and international economic, social, and political development.

Accountability in Health Facilities

PRAEGER SPECIAL STUDIES IN U.S. ECONOMIC, SOCIAL, AND POLITICAL ISSUES

Praeger Publishers   New York   Washington   London

Library of Congress Cataloging in Publication Data

Greenfield, Harry I   1922-
    Accountability in health facilities.

    (Praeger special studies in U. S. economic, social,
and political issues)
    Includes bibliographical references and index.
    1.   Health facilities—United States—Administration.
I.   Title.
RA981.A2G65   658.4'2   75-22233
ISBN 0-275-01310-3

PRAEGER PUBLISHERS
111 Fourth Avenue, New York, N.Y. 10003, U.S.A.

Published in the United States of America in 1975
by Praeger Publishers, Inc.

Printed in the United States of America

From where the community sat, it looked as if its hospital and medical care system had become responsive only to its own expectations. It seemed as if the system had become accountable only to itself.

> Ray E. Brown, "The Hospital and the Community," in The Citizenry and the Hospital, A Report of the 1973 National Forum on the Citizenry and the Hospital, conducted by the Graduate Program in Health Administration of Duke University, Durham, North Carolina, 1974, p. 5.

A democracy is not likely to permit huge and powerful institutions with multiple "spillover" effects on large sections of the population to define their interests in a limited way or to go about pursuing them in a single-minded way. It insists that such institutions show a proper attentiveness to what is conceived to be at any moment, "the public interest."

> Irving Kirstol in The Wall Street Journal, February 14, 1974.

ACKNOWLEDGMENTS

I am indebted to Professor Amitai Etzioni for (at least) three reasons: first his having provided me with the opportunity of working on this project; second his extensive epilogue which provides a conceptual underpinning to the work, and third his constant concern and encouragement.

The Center for Policy Research undertook this study for the Commission on Education for Health Administration with the support of the Kellogg Foundation. Dr. Charles Austin and Ms. Janet Strauss of the Commission subjected the manuscript to a diligent reading and made numerous suggestions which, when they were heeded, helped improve the book as a whole.

I am grateful too to my colleagues and to the staff of the Center for Policy Research for their congeniality and cooperation which in many ways aided both the research and the writing.

A book covering so much territory owes a great deal to the innumerable writers and doers who earlier traversed the ground and who, like the author, are still exploring. My sincere appreciation to one and all.

For any errors or omissions the author alone is responsible and accountable.

The general purposes of the present work are (1) to gather the diverse strands encompassed by the term "accountability" into a more or less coherent form, and (2) to focus the resulting beam on a variety of health facilities in such a way as to illuminate the problem as a whole, and (3) to serve as an input to programs in health administration with a view toward familiarizing present and potential health care administrators with the range of issues involved and with methods of coping, if not of resolution.

According to Webster the adjective accountable is defined as "subject to giving an account; answerable or capable of being accounted for; explainable;" and the noun accountability means the quality or state of being accountable. One should also examine a cognate word, responsibility. Here Webster tells us that the term encompasses moral, legal, or mental accountability; thus the two terms become virtually synonymous. In the present study I differentiate between the two terms: responsibility is viewed as an ex ante concept and accountability is basically ex post. That is to say, a given health facility may assume responsibility for providing care to a predetermined catchment area or population, but the manner in which that responsibility is exercised falls under the rubric of accountability. An institution or administrator cannot and should not be held accountable for activities for which no responsibility was initially assumed. A great deal of confusion will be avoided, we believe, if this distinction is borne in mind.

Another point we should emphasize at the outset is that the present study concerns itself primarily with facilities rather than with personnel. Thus, for example, malpractice suits against individual physicians or dentists in a noninstitutional setting are outside our area of investigation, but when such suits also involve a facility they do fall within our purview.*

---

*For a comprehensive review of some of the points not treated in the present monograph, see Medical Malpractice: The Patient Versus The Physician, A Study submitted by the Subcommittee on Executive Reorganization, Committee on Government Operations, U.S. Senate, Committee Print, 91st. Cong., 1st Sess., November 20, 1969. Also, the British experience is well documented in Rudolf Klein, Complaints Against Doctors: A Study in Professional Accountability (London, Charles Knight, 1973).

This work presented an organizational dilemma: In order to prove useful to present and future administrators in educational programs, a handbook format would probably have been most beneficial; on the other hand, handbooks by their nature require a uniformity and rigidity which is inimical to the present writer's taste and which would prove of more limited value to students of the health field in general. I have attempted therefore to fulfill the requirements of a handbook for ease of reference while simultaneously treating the subject matter in a manner that would also prove of more general value. Accordingly, each of the chapters addresses itself to the various facets of accountability in approximately the following format:

Varieties of Accountability

I.   Internal Accountability
        (a) Legal
        (b) Governance
        (c) Professional
        (d) Flow-of-funds

II.   External Accountability
        (a) Legal
        (b) Governance
        (c) Quality and Functional
        (d) Fiscal and Cost
        (e) Consumer

Internal accountability refers to those aspects of a facility's operation for which, so to speak, it is accountable only to itself; external accountability refers to those aspects of its operations for which a facility, whether for formal (contractual) or informal reasons, is obligated to report to an external, independent agency or group. While the author found this duality convenient for expository purposes, he was not always able to maintain a strict separation between internal and external factors. Hopefully the reader will forgive these transgressions and will believe, with the author, that the substantive issues raised were of greater import than unvarying adherence to the classification scheme.

Despite the humanitarian and nonpecuniary aspects of voluntary hospitals and other health facilities, they have of late been the subject of criticism, vituperation, and even of occupation. Central to the mounting critique is the concept of "accountability." The organization of the present work, as indicated by our format, provides a framework which hopefully will enable us to explore the various facets of the accountability question in a more or less systematic fashion, across many different types of health facilities. We have sought throughout to analyze the operational meanings rather than the abstract concept of the term "accountability," in the belief that this pragmatic approach will prove valuable for policy deliberations as well as for policy modifications.

CONTENTS

List of Abbreviations

AAHA	American Association of Homes for the Aging
AHA	American Hospital Association
AMA	American Medical Association
ANHA	American Nursing Home Association
AUPHA	Association of University Programs in Hospital Administration
CCAHS	Consumer Commission in the Accreditation of Health Services
CHA	Comprehensive Health Audit
C-O-N	Certificate-of-need
CPA	Certified Public Accountant
GAO	General Accounting Office
HEW	Department of Health, Education, and Welfare
HMO	Health Maintenance Organization
HUD	Department of Housing and Urban Development
ICF	Intermediate Care Facility
JCAH	Joint Commission on the Accreditation of Hospitals
MLK	Martin Luther King Jr. Health Clinic
MSO	Medical Staff Organization
NHC	Neighborhood Health Centers
NIMH	National Institute of Mental Health
NYSARC	New York State Association for Retarded Children
OEO	Office of Economic Opportunity
OMB	Office of Management and Budget
OPD	Outpatient Department
PPBS	Planning-Program Budget System
PSRO	Professional Standards Review Organization
QAP	Quality Assurance Program
SNF	Skilled Nursing Facilities
SSA	Social Security Administration
VA	Veterans Administration

1

THE VOLUNTARY
HOSPITAL

A point of departure for almost any study of a segment of our economy is the pivotal question of whether the activity is in the profit or not-for-profit sectors—the latter including governmental as well as nongovernmental functions. In the case of hospitals the answers to this question are relatively straightforward: of the 7,061 hospitals in the United States in 1972, approximately 3,326 or 47 percent fell into the nongovernmental, not-for-profit or voluntary sector; about 2,997 or 42 percent were in the public sector (federal, state and local) and 738 or about 11 percent were in the proprietary area.[1] Along the profit-not-for-profit axis, therefore, close to 90 percent of all hospitals may be said to fall under the latter rubric. Clearly the non-profit milieu is the dominant one in the hospital field—a factor of overriding importance in the analysis of the hospital's role in society.

The present chapter focuses solely on the voluntary, private, not-for-profit hospital.* A quick profile of the voluntary reveals that it is basically a short-term, acute-care facility where the average length of stay in 1972 was eight days. Additionally, voluntaries provided 40 percent of all beds, 66 percent of all admissions, and 51 percent of all outpatient visits during 1972.[2] Moreover, the voluntary hospital has gained in relative importance between 1946 and 1972 with respect to beds, admissions, and outpatient visits.[3] Roughly 90

---

*The term "community hospital" which includes state and local hospitals together with voluntaries is not employed here, since subsequent chapters deal separately with governmental units.

percent of voluntary hospital income is derived from patient revenues, with the remainder attributable to investment income, donations, grants, and other nonmedical services (for example, parking fees, gift shop, cafeteria, and the like). Income from patients, in turn, is divided into "direct-pay" and "third-party" payments (Medicare, Medicaid, Blue Cross, and other insurance). Third-party payments now (1972) account for over 90 percent of total (patient care) revenues. [4]

In order to round out our sketch it may be useful at this point to list the essential characteristics of a general hospital (applicable equally to short and long stays) as set out by the American Hospital Association:[5]

1. The primary function of the institution is to provide diagnostic and treatment services for patients who have a variety of medical conditions, both surgical and nonsurgical.
2. The institution maintains inpatient beds.
3. There is a governing authority legally responsible for the conduct of the institution.
4. There is an administrator to whom the governing authority delegates the full-time responsibility for the operation of the institution in accordance with established policy.
5. There is an organized medical staff to which the governing authority delegates responsibility for maintaining proper standards of medical care.
6. Each patient is admitted on the medical authority of, and is under the supervision of, a member of the medical staff.
7. Registered professional nurse supervision and other nursing services are continuous.
8. A current and complete medical record is maintained for each patient.
9. Pharmacy service is maintained in the institution and is supervised by a registered pharmacist.
10. Diagnostic X-ray service, with facilities and staff for a variety of procedures, is maintained in the institution.
11. Clinical laboratory service, with facilities and staff for a variety of tests and procedures, is maintained in the institution, and anatomical pathology services are regularly and conveniently available.
12. Operating room service, with facilities and staff, is maintained in the institution.
13. Food served to patients meets nutritional requirements, and special diets are regularly available.

These thirteen points outline the structure and function of the prototypical hospital and constitute our frame of reference for the

voluntary hospitals under consideration here. In the remainder of
the present chapter and in the chapters that follow we shall be evaluating the interrelationship between structure and function, paying
particular attention to the junctures at which various groups involved
in the hospital environment are, or are supposed to be, accountable
for their actions. The general definition of accountability that we
follow here is the one put forth by the late Wallace S. Sayre, an
eminent political scientist, who wrote: "The focus is . . . upon the
leadership of the organization, upon its responsibility and accountability for the policies, the performance and the progress of the
organization—an accountability to those who created the organization,
those who support it and those who are served by it . . . "[6]

The expository method employed below was designed to render
the material more tractable and was outlined in the Introduction under
Varieties of Accountability.

INTERNAL ACCOUNTABILITY

Legal Accountability

Voluntary hospitals, like business firms, are creatures of the
law in that they exist by virtue of a charter of incorporation granted
by the Secretary of State of the particular state where the hospital
intends to operate.* The voluntary hospital charter differs from
ordinary business charters, however, in that (a) one of the Articles
of Incorporation specifies that the purposes of the corporation are to
establish and maintain an institution designed to provide patient care,
to carry on educational activities and scientific research associated
with medicine, and to "promote the general health of the community,"[7]
and (b) the statement is made that the corporation "is organized
exclusively for charitable, scientific, and educational purposes as a
not-for-profit corporation; and that its activities shall be conducted
for the aforesaid purposes in such a manner that no part of its net
earnings shall inure to the benefit of any member, director, officer,
or individual."[8] The latter clause entitles the corporation as a

_____

*Corporations which own and operate hospitals in several states
are an exception.

charitable organization to exemption from taxes under section 501 (c)
(3) of the Internal Revenue Code of 1954,[9] as well as under parallel
sections of state and local tax codes.

In her excellent treatment of some of the legal problems arising
from recent trends in hospital affairs, Anne R. Somers[10] points out
that free care is disappearing from hospital service (due principally
to the widespread existence of third-party payments) thus placing in
question the exemption under 501 (c) (3) noted above. The government
has taken advantage of the leverage provided by this development to
induce hospitals to substitute "community services" of one kind or
another in order to retain their exempt status.[11]

Requesting and obtaining a charter, however, is a necessary but
not a sufficient condition for the birth of a hospital. Just as banks
must obtain permission to operate from the State Banking Department
and insurance companies from the State Insurance Department, so too
hospitals are required to obtain a license to operate (operating certificate) and to comply with minimum requirements of the hospital code
promulgated by the State Department of Health. * For instance, Article
2800 of the Public Health Law of the State of New York reads as
follows:[12]

Declaration of Policy and Statement of Purpose

Hospital and related services including health-
related service of the highest quality, efficiently
provided and properly utilized at a reasonable cost,
are of vital concern to the public health. In order to
provide for the protection and promotion of the health
of the inhabitants of the state, pursuant to section three
of article seventeen of the constitution, the department
of health shall have the central, comprehensive responsibility for the development and administration of the
state's policy with respect to hospital and related
services, and all public and private institutions,
whether state, county, minicipal, incorporated or
not incorporated, serving principally as facilities
for the prevention, diagnosis or treatment of human
disease, pain, injury, deformity or physical condition or for the rendering of health-related service
shall be subject to the provisions of this article.

---

*In the case of facilities which receive federal payments (almost
all), the Life Safety Code written into the 1967 Medicaid legislation
also applies.

Almost all of the hospital's professional personnel and many of its allied health workers are likewise subject to state licensure regulations. [13]

Throughout much of our history, licenses to build and operate hospitals were not difficult to obtain provided that the real estate (site) and initial financing factors were present. In fact, only 10 of the 48 states had hospital licensure laws prior to the enactment of the Hill-Burton Act of 1947. [14] A condition for receiving the much needed construction funds provided for by Hill-Burton was (and is) that the hospital's expansion be related to "needs" as determined by a state health planning council. Some states have interpreted the "needs" proviso quite liberally; others, however, have enacted so-called "certificate-of-need" legislation which applies health planning regulations more stringently. For example, a proposed certificate of need act in Illinois would apply to "any capital expenditure of $100,000 or more for expansion, modernization, or new construction" and to "any change in scope of services or functional operation, including termination of a service or facility and change in ownership."[15]

Another aspect of legal accountability concerns the liability of the hospital for acts of negligence occurring within its physical jurisdiction. Here we refer again to the excellent treatment of these matters by Anne Somers. [16] She points out that under the doctrine of "charitable immunity," hospitals were for a long time exempt from ordinary negligence laws. This view was changed, however, primarily by the case of Darling v. Charleston Memorial Hospital (1965), a landmark decision which clearly set out the hospital's corporate responsibility for improper medical treatment of a patient by a physician in the hospital. Even though, technically, the physician was not an employee of the hospital, both he and the hospital were held liable for damages to the patient.

The California Court, in a recent case brought by a patient against both a physician and a hospital (Gonzales v. Nork and Mercy Hospitals) extended the concept of retrospective negligence liability of the hospital (as per the Darling case) to include prospective liability; that is to say, not only is a hospital (and the physician working within its walls) responsible for damage already done to a patient, but also for damage that may be inflicted on a patient in the future by an improperly supervised physician. In the portentous words of the Court, [17]

> The hospital, by virtue of its custody of
> the patient, owes him a duty of care, this
> duty includes the obligation to protect him
> from acts of malpractice by his independ-
> ently retained physician who is a member

of the hospital's staff, if the hospital
knows, or has reason to know, or should
have known that such acts were likely
to occur. . . .

Undoubtedly, every hospital, in an attempt to avoid litigation
under the Nork decision will now attempt to shore up its internal
surveillance procedures as well as to review its procedures for
granting hospital privileges to new physicians. These actions may
not be sufficient, however, for as one writer pointed out, " . . .
delegating authority to its medical staff for performance of specific
quality maintenance functions does not, of itself, relieve a hospital
of its ultimate responsibility."[18]

Governance Accountability

The charter or the bylaws of hospitals specify that the original
incorporators elect a governing board in which the administrative
powers of the corporation shall be vested and "which shall have charge,
control and management of the property, affairs and funds of the
corporation; shall fill vacancies among the officers for unexpired
terms; and shall have the power and authority to do and perform all
acts and functions not inconsistent with these bylaws or with any action
taken by the corporation."[19]

The functions and activities of such governing boards or boards
of trustees are, of course, a locus of a great deal of controversy with
respect to accountability—both internal as well as external. Let us
focus on the former first.

In a fundamental respect, the trustees of a hospital are in the same
predicament as the members of the board of directors of business
corporations. Those groups, other than directors, whose function it
is to carry on the day-to-day and even the longer-run planning activities
of a corporation in an increasingly technologically complex society
gradually assume and come to exercise de facto control—Galbraith's
technostructure, if you will. In the hospital setting, the technostructure
is the medical staff and even though it is the function of the board to
appoint the medical staff and to oversee its activities, it is the latter
group which in fact controls the central aspect of the hospital's
activities—the provision of medical services to patients, and where
applicable, the research and teaching activities of the hospital as well.
A third power center, the administrator of the hospital, is subject to
pressures from the trustees on one side and from the medical staff
on the other—an unenviable position indeed. In larger hospitals, the

nursing staff, which to some extent functions independently of the medical staff, constitutes a fourth locus of control. This quadripartite governance structure, needless to say, can and does generate internal conflict since the respective goals and attitudes of the members of each group often diverge.

For example, the administrator, with an eye on the budget, may be interested in filling beds with any patients; whereas the medical staff, particularly in teaching hospitals, is more concerned with special or interesting cases, or, at the very least, in a wide diversity of case mix. Again, the administrator, still minding the budget, may attempt to induce physicians to order fewer lab tests and X-rays, or to withold purchase of expensive but infrequently used equipment, or to attempt to purchase generic as opposed to brand-name pharmaceuticals—in each of these cases coming into direct conflict with the medical staff. Dr. James G. Haughton, Executive Director of Cook County Hospital, referring to board-staff relations, stated:

> If physicians request an expensive piece of
> equipment, the board members will usually
> approve it, even if the hospital down the
> block has the same piece of equipment,
> because they are public relations conscious.
> There is a greater potential for fund-raising
> and developing nice-looking brochures if there
> is hardware. The board will want to do what
> has "sex appeal"; the members fear that if
> they don't appease their top-flight physicians,
> they will take their patients elsewhere.[20]

Conflicts between the medical staff and trustees may also arise over such issues as the former urging the building of a new wing in a period which the trustees feel may not be propitious for fund raising or borrowing. Then, too, the administration and the board may be at odds over inclusion of the former as a full-fledged board member.

Relationships among the various governance units are, of course, not static, but are influenced by the changing role of the voluntary hospital, changes in financing mechanisms as well as changing requirements of governmental or other agencies. Perrow[21] traced the evolution of the shifting locus of power and control in a voluntary hospital from the trustees, who were the original repositories of control to physicians and finally to the administrator. Herman and Anne Somers also point out that, "The hospital administrator, traditionally an untrained individual content to play a fairly subservient role and socially outranked by doctor and trustee alike, is being transformed into a professional with increasing self-confidence and authority.[22] (The activities of the American College of Hospital Administrators and the Association of University Programs in Hospital Administration have played seminal roles in upgrading the position of the administrator in the hospital hierarchy.)

While acknowledging the growing importance of the administrator, our earlier statement concerning the power of the technostructure still holds. One author noted that the trustees, "almost invariably" side with the medical staff in cases of intergroup conflict.[23]

Roemer and Friedman[24] present a slightly different view of the lines of authority but basically support the Kaitz position:

> General hospitals of the United States are typically characterized by two lines of internal authority: the medical and the administrative. While theoretically the medical staff comes under the supervision of the hospital board of directors, its latitude for decisions tends to be very wide. Since most general hospital patients are under the private care of an individual physician, he has the greatest legal and moral responsibility for patient care. Limitations and restrictions on his behavior are imposed by an organization of the medical staff itself and only indirectly by the board of directors. There are usually rather strict limitations to the responsibility of the hospital administrator—who is nearly always a nonmedical man—despite his being the agent of the board of directors.

Professional Accountability

The power and influence of each of the major groups is limited not only by shifting intergroup relationships but also by other factors. First among these is self-image. Next come the standards set by the professional associations of which they are members. Third are the limitations and responsibilities of the occupation as set forth by various licensing bodies. This implies that administrative directives from the various power centers mentioned (which are, or are interpreted to be, at variance with either professional self-image or with the dictates of professional organizations or with the boundaries of the license itself)

may be resisted or abrogated entirely, thereby generating additional
potential conflicts within the hospital structure. Nor should one omit
the influence of increasing unionization of hospital workers. As in
the business sector, union rules and regulations place additional limits
on managerial prerogatives. Virtually all hospital personnel are therefore to some degree "accountable" to themselves as members of a
profession as well as to a variety of bodies within and outside of the
hospital walls.

Roemer and Friedman cite an early (1913) example of the way
in which an external professional association (the American College
of Surgeons) influenced internal professional standards:[25]

> In order to establish a basis of merit for member-
> ship in this private professional society, the College
> required that each candidate submit 100 complete
> medical records of patients on whom he had
> operated, demonstrating thereby his technical
> ability and judgment. It was soon discovered,
> however, that few applicants could comply with
> this requirement.

Besides the early work of the American College of Surgeons, the same
authors also traced the roles of the Council on Medical Education of
the American Medical Association in standardizing internship and
residency training. At this point the demarcation between internal
and external accountability becomes blurred. The standardization
movement for present purposes may be viewed as setting goals for
individual performance apart from those set by external groups of
one kind or another.

As early as 1928, T. R. Ponton stated that it was an obligation
of every hospital to police itself—an early call for what has since come
to be known as "peer review."[26] The degree to which internal professional accountability is obtained by peer review has, however, been
called into question. Howard and Martha Lewis[27] wrote recently that:

> In most accredited hospitals, a physician's
> qualifications are systematically reviewed
> only when he applies for privileges. There-
> after, his performance may be reviewed while
> he is still new to the staff. Checking on ap-
> plicants is a function of the Credentials
> Committee, which is often the only active
> disciplinary committee in the hospitals.

These authors maintain that in both small as well as large hospitals
and in both good and bad hospitals, there is generally a reluctance
on the part of medical staffs to discipline their colleagues. Moreover,
say the Lewises, underscoring Haughton's observations cited earlier, [28]

> Discipline may (also) be obstructed by the board
> of trustees which governs the corporation control-
> ling the hospital and by the administrator—the
> hospital's chief executive, usually a layman,
> who reports to the board. If the trustees and
> the administrator are overconcerned with
> finances, they may reject the medical staff's
> disciplinary recommendation against a doctor
> who brings a large number of patients into the
> institution. If they are too mindful of politics,
> they may not care to offend a physician who is
> influential in the community.

More will be said below concerning the raising of professional
standards within the hospital through the activities of the Joint
Commission on the Accreditation of Hospitals—an external, voluntary
control, (not a licensing) body.

The pinnacle of the long evolution of internal professional accountability is reached by the development of the Quality Assurance Program
(QAP) of the American Hospital Association. Since this program was
built out of previous efforts, no specific date can be supplied for its
origin. The quote freom the foreword of the descriptive QAP com-
pilation, [29]

> It is a primary premise of this document that a hospital
> cannot abdicate its primary responsibility for conducting
> its own in-house quality assurance program. Legal prec-
> edent would appear to support the principle that a hospital
> board of trustees has the ultimate responsibility to assure
> the quality of all care provided within the institution—a
> responsibility it cannot delegate. However, it is legal
> for the board to share the responsibility for the conduct
> of this program to those over whom it has the authority
> and to those who are accountable to the board for the
> performance of the program and to delegate requisite
> authority for this purpose. Out-of-hospital surveil-
> lance programs as anticipated in pending legislation
> [such as, Professional Standards Review Organizations]
> should not be substituted as an alternative to this program.

The hospital quality assurance program is a program designed to improve quality of care; surveillance is a necessary but limited part of the total program that is designed to bring about change primarily through continuing education.

The rather thick loose-leaf compendium then describes in detail the major components of a quality assurance program, which consists of two main thrusts: (1) a utilization review program designed to monitor hospital utilization patterns such as admissions, length of stay, and discharges, and (2) a medical audit program designed to measure the care received by professional standards. This includes the work previously done by tissue and medical records committees and the like.

No indication is given of the extent to which the QAP program has been adopted and/or implemented in member (AHA) hospitals.

Internal Flow-of-Funds Accountability

Some elementary kinds of financial and managerial controls can be expected of any organization which receives and dispenses funds. The hospital in its day-to-day functioning incurs costs both operating and capital; revenues, as stated earlier, are derived from patient care, from philanthropy, and from government. As a matter of necessity as well as of law, annual balance sheets and income statements will be drawn up. * In addition, well-run hospitals, and even others, attempt financial management via the budgetary process. In the words of Klarman, [30]

> Most voluntary hospitals in New York City have a budget. The budget of a hospital is peculiarly its own and reflects its special circumstances. After approval by the board of trustees, it becomes a flexible plan for spending in the coming year and can serve as a vehicle for management

---

*Some firms specialize in hospital accounting exclusively or have developed large departments within their organizations for this purpose.

control. Thus, although not every voluntary
hospital has a formal budget and although not
every hospital with a budget employs it as a
tool of management, many hospitals do both
and no hospital that wishes to adopt these
practices is precluded from so doing.

In a profit-seeking firm, it is top management's responsibility
(to the board, which, in turn, is theoretically accountable to public
shareholders, if any) to minimize costs and to maximize revenues,
thereby maximizing profits or minimizing losses. Market pressures
and shareholder expectations and demands are the mechanisms
which insure that profit considerations (for the short and longer run)
have a high if not the highest priority in guiding managerial decisions.
Such mechanisms, while not wholly absent, are nonetheless largely
inoperative in the not-for-profit hospital. One author, for instance,
who sent a detailed questionnaire to a sample of hospitals in Massachusetts, reported that "All of the administrators included in this
study thought that neither price nor cost is an appropriate benchmark
for decision making in the hospital industry, even though they used
both of these financial figures. Each administrator maintained that
because human lives are involved, the hospital must provide the best
care possible, regardless of cost."[31]

One of the major points of Kaitz's book is that the cost-plus method
of reimbursement (to the hospital by insurance carriers) which has,
until recently, been universally prevalent in the hospital field, reinforced the administrator's lack of concern with costs and managerial efficiency.

Another question raised by Kaitz which is germane here concerns
the locus of responsibility and accountability for the internal flow of
funds in hospitals. He writes:[32]

This raises the subtle issue of the true managerial authority of the hospital administrator.
In general, this writer believes, the authority
of the administrator is pretty well denigrated
by the general organization of most voluntary
hospitals. For the most part, the board of
trustees tends to limit the adminstrator's
authority by over-controlling the number
and quality of decisions that it must ratify.
By assuming authority for most financial
decisions, the trustees relieve the administration of the bulk of his executive responsibility for directing the activities of

the hospital. Therefore, the adminstrations
do not appear to be greatly concerned with
the financial integrity of the hospital. In
general, they conveyed the impression to
this writer that this was the direct, day-
to-day responsibility of the board.

In the absence of evidence from a broader sample of hospitals,
one would assume that the extent to which trustees become involved
in daily financial decisions is a function primarily of the size of the
hospital and, secondarily, of the abilities and standing of the administrator himself. The likelihood is that in larger, multidepartmental
hospitals, it is the administrators who would assume responsibility
for daily or short-term fiscal matters, while the trustees will be
involved in financial decisions of a longer-run nature. [33]

Due to the rapidity with which hospital costs have been rising,
increasing attention is being paid by government, the "blues,"—
commercial insurance carriers—and employers to the potential
for ameliorating cost inflation by the use of prospective (as opposed
to retrospective) reimbursement, and by the application of industrial
management techniques designed to increase internal efficiency and
productivity. [34]

As in the case of specialized hospital accounting firms mentioned
earlier, specialized hospital consulting firms as well as individual
hospital consultants have been increasingly employed to study hospital
systems and to suggest improvements. A whole range of techniques
first applied to industrial concerns, such as operations research,
Planning-Program Budget Systems (PPBS), cost-benefit analysis,
and linear programming have been utilized (with what success is not
widely known) in the analysis of hospital activities. It appears that
with increasing outside scrutiny and pressure, rigidities and archaic
practices which hindered the attainment of intrahospital efficiency are
not as powerful and pervasive as they once were. However, the present
writer's finding of decreases in output per employee in a sample of
New York hospitals over the 1960-70 decade, indicates that much
remains to be accomplished in this area. [35]

EXTERNAL ACCOUNTABILITY

Legal Accountability

Throughout our history it has generally been understood, though
not necessarily written into law, that the nature of hospital services
renders it an activity "affected with the public interest." Several

current cases may be cited where in fact the traditional view has become, as it were, statutized. In an informative study Gladys A. Harrison commented:[36]

> A general statement on the present-day
> status of the private (voluntary) nonprofit
> community hospital, contained in a memo-
> randum filed by the United States as amicus
> curiae in a recent case in the federal district
> court in North Carolina bids fair to become
> classic: the memorandum asserts broadly
> that, "it is particularly appropriate to view
> a nonprofit hospital as an institution affected
> with a public interest."

Again, Anne Somers cites the case of Grusman v. Newcomb Hospital, where the court held that "a voluntary hospital is vested with a public interest and should not be treated strictly as a private organization, at least when it is the sole hospital in the immediate geographic area."[37] The same author also quotes Professor Southwick to the effect that "a voluntary hospital is never truly private in character and outreach. It is perfectly evident that social and economic factors shape law and policy; the result is that the nonprofit hospital must consider itself to be a public or quasi-public institution."[38]

The legal position of hospitals as semipublic institutions is buttressed by the fact that there is also a huge public investment in hospitals through construction and equipment grants, research funds, and indirectly through tax exemption. As a quid pro quo, hospitals— albeit reluctantly—have had to subject themselves to increasing public regulation, and some authorities support the view that voluntary hospitals are in actuality public utilities and should be similarly regu- lated.[39]

Governance Accountability

One of the ways of gauging the extent to which the voluntary hospital's management considers itself to be (or reacts to external views of itself as being) a quasi-public institution is the presence or absence of representatives of the "public" on its governing board. The "public" member may be a government official (one who may have been elected or appointed or a career civil servant), or he may be a rep- resentative of the public-at-large, who is a potential consumer of the hospital's services and who has no connection with the existing board members—a situation not unlike the outside director on business boards. By this measure of public representation, voluntary hospitals in general receive low grades.

The closest approach to a national survey of the composition of, and methods of election to, hospital governing boards is a study that appeared in Hospitals in 1972.[40] The first question to which the authors of the report sought an answer was whether boards were "self-perpetuating," that is, whether board members were elected by the boards themselves. While the authors concluded that their survey "demonstrates that most hospital governing boards are not self-perpetuating,"[41] their conclusion is not supported by the underlying data. In the first place, the authors made a distinction between "board elected" and "corporate elected" (the latter denoting election by a body separate from the board in which ultimate legal accountability resides). This appears to the present writer as a purely legalistic distinction lacking any substantive difference. Since the original board was elected by the "incorporators" (who, incidentally, are not responsible to shareholders or to any other group) it is not unreasonable to assume that (a) either the same criteria will be employed in filling vacancies, or that (b) the board itself will present to the "corporation" the names of those it wishes to be elected. True, the "corporation" has de jure status but the de facto control by the trustees means that in practice, the two bodies function as one. If this is the case, then board membership should be judged to be self-perpetuating in almost 80 percent of the voluntary hospitals in the survey. In fact, only 7 percent of board members were found to be in the category "elected by other group," and we are not told the nature of these other groups.[42]

The second major question of the same survey concerned the occupational classification of board members. Here too the authors indicated that their survey "disproved . . . some of the myths concerning the careers of hospital board members."[43] When the data clearly show that (1) "persons in executive, managerial and white-collar capacities constitute the largest single group of hospital governing board members"[44] and that (2) "professionals from the community, including judges, attorneys, college presidents, ambassadors and teachers, are the second largest career group on hospital boards,"[45] and further that (3) "less than one percent of the total board membership in reporting hospitals are blue-collar workers,"[46] it is difficult to comprehend what "myths" were disproved.

An earlier study of hospital board composition in a sample of Detroit hospitals[47] showed a preponderance of "business" and "non-health professional" representation on not-for-profit boards, 58.5 and 14.7 percent, respectively—a total of 63.2 percent. The authors of that study concluded:[48]

> Hospital boards are dominated by business
> executives, members of the legal and account-
> ing professions and spokesmen for medicine
> and hospitals. Representatives of the consumer
> and the general community are very seriously
> underrepresented. Obviously, hospital boards
> are not representative of nor do they reflect
> the composition of the community generally.

A third study of hospital governing boards—this one from a sample
of hospitals in the Greater Boston area[49]—produced much the same
profile of hospital trustees, as did the others. The authors of this
study stated:[50]

> The observation of hospital board member
> occupations in Boston are almost identical
> to those of Goldberg and Hemmelgarn in
> Detroit, who reported that hospital boards
> there are dominated by business executives,
> members of the legal and accounting profes-
> sions, and representatives from medicine
> and hospital administration. In regard to the
> communities served, there is an apparent
> underrepresentation of the low- and median-
> income health consumers both in Detroit and
> Boston.

A fourth study of hospital board members, this one from a sample
of Long Island hospitals,[51] indicated that the four largest occupational
categories were as follows (in percent):[52]

Corporate business	16.0
M.D.s	15.3
Banking	10.7
Small business	10.5
Law	9.5
	61.5

These results also conform rather closely to those of the previous
studies. An additional statistic provided in the Munk-Saffier study
raises the sex issue: 92.4 percent of board members were male.

The results of these four studies of hospital board compositon
are as alike as they are not surprising. An examination of the questions
of whether the occupational mix of existing boards is dysfunctional
from the point of view of hospital behavior, of actual and potential

conflict of interest, of the role of consumers on boards, and of various proposals for changes in board structure and function is deferred to our concluding chapter.

Functional and Quality Accountability

We have discussed some of the ways in which the concepts and applications of internal professional accountability developed. Here we take up the interrelated questions of functional and quality accountability which are externally imposed on the hospital. No implication is made that hospitals generally resist such imposition; concern here is with the direction (and hence the initiative) from which these types of accountability originate.

Hospitals, let us recall, until relatively recently were established and grew without any planning constraints or even licensure requirements from either national, state, or local bodies.* As one might expect, the types of activities undertaken by these hospitals were likewise haphazard, being influenced more by the availability of particular physicians and by the need for revenue rather than by the studied needs of potential in- or outpatients. Hospitals, in short, were not accountable to any external body for their programs.

The movement for quality control under the aegis of the American College of Surgeons, the requirements laid down by the American Medical Association for the education of interns and residents as well as the long-standing concern for upgrading standards on the part of the American Hospital Association, gradually brought about the notion of what functions a general hospital should perform (p. 2) and what proficiency levels should be sought. These correlates of function and quality have become formalized into "Approvals" and "Affiliations" and are reported on annually by the American Hospital Association. The most recent such listing is shown in Appendix A, Table A-2).

----

*An interesting case concerning the expansion of a hospital over the opposition of a state planning board, but with a $62 million Federal loan guarantee, is that of the Cedars of Lebanon Hospital of Miami, Times, April 15, 1974. The hospital, by the way, is now bankrupt.

It should be noted that all of the approvals and affiliations are granted by external agencies (only 1 out of 9 is governmental) and further, that the individual hospital voluntarily applies for such approvals or linkages. On the basis of these indicators of quality, American hospitals in general do not fare very well. The voluntary hospitals exceed the averages in each case, but it must be admitted that 17 percent rates for Cancer Programs and Internships, an 11 percent rate for Medical School affiliation, and even the 21 percent rate for Residencies are disappointingly low. The very high rates for Blue Cross and Medicare participation are of course a reflection of the need for funds by the hospitals, and (one must surmise) of the relative ease of meeting the requirements for participation in these programs.

Over the last decade or so the Joint Commission on the Accreditation of Hospitals (JCAH) has emerged as the major internal agency which through its process of granting "accreditation" status, aims to upgrade and maintain quality standards. To quote from JCAH's Accreditation Manual for Hospitals,[53]

> The purposes of the Joint Commission on Accreditation of Hospitals which have remained in effect as its fundamental guidelines since its incorporation in 1952 are:
> 1. To establish standards for the operation of hospitals and other health care facilities and services.
> 2. To conduct survey and accreditation programs that will encourage members of the health professions, hospitals and other health care facilities and services voluntarily to:
>   a. Promote high quality of care in all aspects in order to give patients the optimal benefits that medical science has to offer;
>   b. Apply certain basic principles of physical plant safety and maintenance, and of organization and administration of function for efficient care of patient;
>   c. Maintain the essential services in the facilities through coordinated effort of the organized staffs and the governing bodies of the facilities.

We noted earlier that seeking JCAH accreditation is voluntary on the part of health facilities. However, since the 1965 Amendments to the Social Security Act stipulated that JCAH accreditation, or its equivalent, is mandatory for the participation of health facilities in the Medicare program, the JCAH has, in the words of one writer, been "cast into an entirely new role as a quasi-public licensing body."[54]

Proprietary hospitals and extended care facilities of all kinds will be found generally to have low rates of accreditation (see Appendix A, Table A-2), either because they do not seek it or because they do not offer a full range of required services. Mention should be made here of the fact that there are provisions for community inputs to the JCAH accreditation survey teams, but more on this in Chapter 6.

Apart from hospitals' own desires to improve quality and programs in order to satisfy external agencies such as JCAH, is the assumption of certain specified functions under the pressure of financial leverage exerted by fund sources. For example, the Hill-Burton Act of 1946 " . . . provided for a reasonable amount of free or below-cost patient care to be provided by grantee hospitals unless there was an explicit waiver of this provision based on financial hardship of the grantee institution."[55] Lawyers associated with the National Health and Environmental Law Program of the University of California Law School utilized this provision which, to their knowledge, " . . . had not been enforced during the twenty-five years of the administration of the program," to enforce compliance with the law. One important outcome of the litigation was to induce the Department of Health, Education, and Welfare, to promulgate clearer guidelines as to what constitutes free or below-cost care as per the Hill-Burton statute. The following extended comment by Mr. Silver, one of the attorneys involved concerning the use of legal responsibility and accountability, is instructive:[56]

> We have been recognizing—sometimes belatedly and sorrowfully—that courts may not be the appropriate forums for achieving wide-sweeping social change, and assuredly courts cannot legislate a solution to the problem of financing the medical care of the non-categorically related medical indigent. Yet we have seen the use of the courts—in dealing with the non-responsiveness and non-accountability of monopolistic enterprises (governmental agencies and not-for-profit hospitals, for example)—to prod, push, and shove vulnerable parts of the system. Then the vulnerable parts of the system—the hospitals—can rethink new solutions to a system's problem. Where other avenues of increasing accountability do not work, where there are not mechanisms of restraint imposed upon the system by competitive forces, the courts can perform a useful function in getting hospital officials to honor the commitments which they perhaps heedlessly made, regarding the requirement to provide free or below cost services to the indigent as "boiler plate" language in the contract.

Fiscal and Cost Accountability

The reasons for escalating hospital costs are complex and have
been the subject of investigation by many authors and groups beginning
with the now classic studies in the early 1930s by the Committee on
the Costs of Medical Care.[57] Despite the plethora of studies, no group
evolved analogous to the JCAH whose major function would have been
to monitor the costs of production of health services—on the order of,
say, a Joint Commission on Hospital Costs. Even though hospital
revenues customarily fell short of hospital expenses, resulting in
chronic deficit operations, attention of the public became increasingly
focused on the levels of those costs and expenses—particularly in the
mid-1950s when they began to accelerate more rapidly than consumer
prices generally.[58] This public concern generated a large number of
studies and conferences, the most important of which were the New
York State, "Report of the Governor's Committee on Hospital Costs"
(1965); the Report of a Conference Convened by the National Academy
of Engineering; "Costs of Health Care Facilities" (1968), The Gorham
Report to the President, "Medical Care Prices" (1967); the "Report
of the National Conference on Medical Costs" (1967); the Barr Committee Report titled "Secretary's Advisory Committee on Hospital
Effectiveness" (1968) and Hearings before the Subcommittee on Anti-
trust and Monopoly of the United States Senate on "The High Cost of
Hospitalization" (1970).
Many of these reports focused on managerial inefficiency and
most of them dealt at length with methods of reimbursement of hospitals
by third parties as causal factors in the inflation process. The vast
increase in federal and state outlays for hospital care occasioned by
the addition of Title 18 and 19 (Medicare and Medicaid) to the Social
Security law (1965) spurred additional investigations into hospital
operations and costs, notably the Hearings before the Subcommittee
on Medicare-Medicaid of the Committee on Finance of the United
States Senate (1970) and the Report of the Task Force on Medicaid
and Related Programs (1970).[59]
In general, the results of these investigations have been meager.
Some states now require uniform financial reporting by hospitals; a
few states (New York, Connecticut, and Massachusetts) have actually
adopted so-called hospital cost control laws; Blue Cross Associations
and other carriers are experimenting with new reimbursement techniques, and the federal government states that it will pay only "reasonable and customary" costs for the care of patients under Medicare
and Medicaid. Legislation designed to encourage the formation of Health
Maintenance Organizations (HMOs) has been passed with the hope that

costs may be abated and quality raised; the same holds true for
professional standards review organizations which are rapidly
forming.

Withal, it is interesting to note that hospital costs continued
their upward climb and began to abate only when price controls were
imposed nationally under the Economic Stabilization Program.[60]
Significantly, "inflation-prone" hospital costs were the last to be
decontrolled when the wage-price ceilings were in the process of
being phased out.[61] Again, we defer to Chapter 6 a consideration of
suggestions for enhancing accountability for hospital costs and prices.

Consumer Accountability

The growing incidence of malpractice suits brought against individual physicians and the expected increase in such suits brought
against hospitals as a consequence of the Darling and Nork decisions
cited above brings a new sense of urgency to questions of responsibility
and accountability to consumers of health services. These suits are
predicated on the responsibility that providers of health care have
to render care that meets high (though not the highest) standards.
Moreover, the standards are not local ones, but are increasingly
regional and national in scope.

It is generally recognized that the caveat emptor precept is largely
inapplicable in the health care field. In ordinary market activity, the
concept of consumer sovereignty, though it has come in for some heavy
blows recently from Galbraith and Nader, retains some viability—a
viability that is in direct proportion to consumer knowledge (and income). If one knows with certainty that car A is better than car B
(in respect to quality and/or price), it would take a tremendous amount
of financial resources for the producer of car B to change the consumer's mind.* It is precisely the lack of knowledge by consumers
concerning the quality of health care and the virtual lack of control
over the quantity purchased—the latter because consumer demand
operates indirectly through surrogates (the physician and the hospital),

---

*In the market, for most goods and services, advertising attempts
to, and often succeeds in influencing consumer demand; in the health
field, neither physicians nor hospitals advertise.

that producer rather than consumer sovereignty may be said to prevail. (Various techniques designed to increase consumer knowledge in health are discussed in Chapter 6.)

What of responsibility and accountability in the positive sense? For voluntary hospitals, this would take the form of assuring consumers that care is always accessible, that it will be of the appropriate kind and quality, and that it will be rendered efficiently, with dignity, under pleasant surroundsing, and at the lowest possible cost. In addition, the expressed desires of consumers for new health programs or for modifications of existing ones will be given the same serious consideration as is now given to a request from the Chief of Medical Service or of a trustee. Finally, one would expect that constructive criticism of existing practices will result in appropriate behavior modification on the part of the institution and of its personnel. A mere exposition of these correlates of consumer responsibility and accountability should be sufficient to indicate their general absence from the hospital field. [62]

Some of the above listed attributes are undoubtedly present in some hospitals, but it would be difficult to cite a single case of their collective presence. However, things are changing. The voluntary hospital, although it possesses a great deal of autonomy, nevertheless does not function in a vacuum. The rise of "consumerism," the movement for "community control," the passage of new federal legislation which conditions payment for health services to vendors on, among other things, "consumer representation," have had and continue to have their effects.

The winds of consumerism were undoubtedly partially responsible for the adoption by the Board of Trustees of the American Hospital Association in 1972 of a "Statement on a Patient's Bill of Rights" (reproduced in Appendix A). The twelve-point program reverses the traditional medical mystique which holds that the patient who knows least is the best. Each of the points begins with the phrase, "The patient has the right . . . ", and the entire bill represents a high point in hospital and physician accountability to inpatients. There is no comparable statement, however, with respect to hospitals' responsibility and accountability to outpatients, to potential patients, and to the community in general for preventive health care, or for economy in operation.

An informative tabulation by the Community Health Institute of New York[63] lists several federal, state, and city statutes which mandate consumer participation in health care. Some examples may be instructive here. The Comprehensive Health Planning and Public Health Services Act of 1966 (PL89-749) which aims at raising the level and efficiency of health planning in states requires that a majority of members of the state health planning council must be "consumer

representatives." The same stipulation holds for regional planning
bodies with the additional proviso that such bodies must include
minority group representatives who reside in the area in question,
and who "must be acceptable to the community." Health planning, it
should be noted, encompasses the building of new health facilities as
well as the expansion or modification of existing ones.

A New York State statute known as the "Ghetto Medicine Act"
which provides subsidies to voluntary hospitals that provide ambulatory
services to low-income patients, requires each hospital to have an
ambulatory care advisory committee, the majority of whom "must be
consumers."

Since the Hill-Burton Act required the setting up of state planning
agencies and since these agencies are now (or are supposed to be)
"consumer-dominated," hospitals receiving Hill-Burton funds presumably have consumer accountability incorporated into their plans
for the disposition of said funds. Similarly, although there is no
specific provision for consumer participation in the Social Security
Administration manual outlining "Conditions of Participation for
Hospitals" in the Medicare and Medicaid programs, the fact that their
programs rely on the state administrative apparatus and that hospitals
are required to comply with state and local law, implies that some
consumer input will be present as a factor affecting the huge fund
flows occasioned by these Acts.

Further, a recent article on consumerism in health noted that,
"Under a law passed last year (1972), the department [HEW] if it
finds substantial complaints about a hospital, can undertake its own
independent accreditation survey under the authority granted to it
in dispensing funds."[64] Illustrating a point that was mentioned earlier
with respect to consumer input to the accreditation surveys of JCAH,
the same article states that, "Consumer involvement was a factor
(yesterday) when the Joint Commission, in issuing its recommendations
for the Nassau County Medical Center, incorporated a number of points
raised by Community Advocates, a public interest consumer group.
These included proposals for more doctors to handle the outpatient
load, for confidentiality and privacy in outpatient service and for
interpreters to aid doctors and foreign-speaking patients."[65]

CONCLUSION

The not-for-profit, community-service aura surrounding the
voluntary hospital has, it would seem, acted as a shield which for
a long time has insulated such hospitals from governmental regulatory
agencies on the one hand, and from (largely unorganized) consumer

groups, on the other. Insurance carriers have played a neutral role
which, in this case, has reinforced the hospital's independence by
virtue of the financial solvency they provided. The present chapter
has touched on some of the formal and informal accountability mechanisms which have either recently evolved, (such as Professional
Standards Review Organizations or PSROs), or which have, under
various current pressures, undergone revitalization, like JCAH. It
is of course not possible to quantify, by means of an "accountability
index," the extent to which voluntary hospitals are more accountable
now than, say, ten years ago. Rapidly rising health care costs (especially hospital rates); increasing involvement of the federal government via Medicare, Medicaid, and (imminently) with some variety of
national health insurance; the assumption by insurance carriers of a
greater role in cost and quality surveillance, increasing concern
within the medical professions with external interference and a growing
consumer movement, [66]—all of these factors point to placing accountability questions in the forefront of the debates on the future of the
health care delivery system. In our concluding chapter we will point
to those kinds of mechanisms for accountability (some discussed in
the present chapter and new ones as well) which have greater potential
for achieving their goal in the voluntary hospital milieu than do others.

NOTES

    1. Hospital Statistics, 1972 American Hospital Association,
Chicago, 1973, Table 1. Some estimation was necessary since break-
downs by proprietary and state and local facilities are not provided
in the nonfederal psychiatric, nonfederal tuberculous, and nonfederal
long-term general and other special categories.
    2. Ibid.
    3. See Appendix A, Table A-1.
    4. "The Size and Shape of the Medical Care Dollar," Chart Book,
1972, Social Security Administration, Department of Health, Education,
and Welfare Publication No. SSA 73-11910, p. 23.
    5. Classification of Health Care Institutions (Chicago: American
Hospital Association, 1968), p. 14.
    6. Wallace S. Sayre, "Principles of Administration—2, Hospitals
30 (February 1956) 51. See also David D. Henry, "Accountability:
To Whom, For What, By What Means?," Educational Record 53 no.
4 (Fall 1972) pp. 287 ff.
    7. Guide for Preparation of Constitution and By-laws for General
Hospitals (Chicago: American Hospital Association, 1973), pp. 5-7.
    8. Ibid.

9. Two examples may be cited here: Article II of the Constitution of the Beth Israel Hospital Association in New York states that the hospital proposes "To give medical and surgical aid, nursing and dispensary service, and medical-social service to the sick or disabled, to give prenatal, obstetrical and postpartum care to women, and to cooperate with health and welfare organizations in the prevention of disease, all toward the service of humanity in accord with the highest ideals of medical science. . . . To provide the services of this institution to poor people free of charge, regardless of race, color, creed or nationality. . . . In furtherance of the foregoing objects, to make the services of this institution available to persons who are able to pay therefor in order to help defray the cost of providing its services to the poor." Similarly, the preamble to the Restated Certificates of Incorporation of St. Vincent's Hospital and Medical Center of New York (as of June 28, 1973) states that certain specified persons, " . . . desire to and hereby do associate ourselves for the charitable purposes hereinafter stated . . . " and further that said persons desire "to make available optimal patient care with continuity of service for the sick poor and disabled and all others without regard to race, color or creed, by means of prevention, diagnosis, treatment rehabilitation and/or home care for hospitalized and ambulatory patients."

10. Anne R. Somers, Hospital Regulation: The Dilemma of Public Policy (Princeton, N.J.: Princeton University, Industrial Relations Section, Research Report Series No. 112 1969), chap. 3 and passim. See also Milton I. Roemer and Jay W. Friedman, Doctors in Hospitals, (Baltimore: Johns Hopkins Press, 1971), particularly chap. 1.

11. Ibid., pp. 49, 52-53.

12. Excerpted from Materials on Health Law prepared by the Health Law Project, University of Pennsylvania Law School, vol. 2, rev. ed. (1972), p. 465.

13. M. Y. Pennell and P. A. Stewart, State Licensing of Health Occupations, Department of Health, Education, and Welfare, Public Health Service Publication No. 1758, Washington, D.C., 1968, and the companion report, State Licensing of Health Facilities, DHEW Public Health Service Publication No. 1757, 1968.

14. Roemer and Friedman, op. cit., p. 39.

15. "Is 'Certificate of Need' Needed?," Medical World News, August 24, 1973.

16. Somers, op. cit., pp. 103-104. See also Gladys O. Harrison, Government Controls and the Voluntary Nonprofit Hospital (Chicago: American Hospital Association, 1961), pp. 30-33, especially supplementary statement on external voluntary controls affecting hospitals.

17. Cited in "Court Decision Would Extend Liability," Hospitals 48, no. 2 (January 16, 1974), p. 31.

18. Ibid., p. 33.

19. Guide For Preparation of Constitution and By-laws for General Hospitals, op. cit., p. 11.

20. "Is 'Certificate of Need' Needed?," op. cit., p. 87.

21. Charles B. Perrow, "Goals and Power Structures", in Eliot Freidson, ed., The Hospital in Modern Society (New York: Free Press, 1963), p. 114.

22. Herman M. Somers and Anne R. Somers, Doctors, Patients and Health Insurance (Washington, D.C.: Brookings Institution, 1961), p. 68. See also Lowell E. Bellin, "The Health Administrator as Status Seeker," Journal of Medical Education 48 (October 1973).

23. Edward M. Kaitz, Pricing Policy and Cost Behavior in the Hospital Industry (New York: Praeger Publishers, 1968), p. 95.

24. Roemer and Friedman, op. cit., pp. 50-51.

25. Ibid., p. 35.

26. Materials on Health Law, op. cit., p. 232. See also Peer Review Manual (Chicago: American Medical Association, 1971) and Utilization Review, A Handbook for the Medical Staff (Chicago: American Medical Association, 1965).

27. Howard Lewis and Martha Lewis, The Medical Offenders (New York: Simon and Schuster, Inc., 1970), p. 66.

28. Ibid., p. 69.

29. Quality Assurance Program for Medical Care in the Hospital (Chicago: American Hospital Association, 1972), p. 1. (Emphasis in original.)

30. Herbert E. Klarman, Hospital Care in New York City (New York: Columbia University Press, 1963), p. 278.

31. Kaitz, op. cit., p. 65. See also Harry I. Greenfield Hospital Efficiency and Public Policy (New York: Praeger Publishers, 1973), passim.

32. Ibid., p. 66.

33. Frederick C. LeRocker and Kenneth P. Howard, "What Decisions do Trustees Actually Make?" The Modern Hospital, April 1960.

34. Harry I. Greenfield, op. cit., chap. 4.

35. Ibid., p. 36.

36. Gladys O. Harrison, Control of Medical Staff Appointments in Voluntary Nonprofit Hospitals (Chicago: American Hospital Association, 1963), p. 4.

37. Somers, op. cit., p. 24, and other cases cited therein.

38. Ibid., p. 25.

39. See the discussion of this issue in Herbert E. Klarman, The Economics of Health (New York: Columbia University Press, 1965), pp. 147-148; also Somers, op. cit., pp. 204-208; and in Greenfield, op. cit., p. 62.

40. Kay Gilmore and John R. Wheeler, "A National Profile of Governing Boards," Hospitals 46 (November 1, 1972).

41. Ibid., p. 108.

42. Ibid., Table 1, p. 105.

43. Ibid., p. 106.

44. Ibid., p. 108.

45. Ibid.

46. Ibid.

47. Theodore Goldberg and Ronald Hemmelgarn, "Who Governs Hospitals," Hospitals 45 (August 1, 1971), Part 1.

48. Ibid., p. 79.

49. Ian Berger and Robert Earsy, "Occupations of Boston Hospital Board Members," Inquiry 10, no. 1 (March 1973).

50. Ibid., p. 45.

51. Michael Munk and Ken Saffier, "Who Governs Long Island Hospitals?," 1973 (mimeo).

52. Ibid., Table III, p. 8; particularly chap. 2, pp. 28-37.

53. "Accreditation Manual for Hospitals, 1970" (updated 1973), Hospital Accreditation Program, Joint Commission on Accreditation of Hospitals, Chicago. See also "Trustee, Administrator, Physician (TAP) Institutes," published under the same auspices.

54. Carl B. Schlicke, "American Surgery's Noblest Experiment," Archives of Surgery 106 (April 1973), cited in "TAP Institutes."

55. Laurens H. Silver, "Legal Accountability of Not-for-Profit Hospitals," paper prepared for Conference on Health Planning, Certificates of Need, and Market Entry, held at American Enterprise Institute for Public Policy Research, Washington, D.C., June 15-16, 1972, p. 3.

56. Ibid., p. 10.

57. See Medical Care for the American People, Final Report of the Committee on the Costs of Medical Care, adopted in Washington, D.C., October 31, 1932 (reprinted 1970 by Department of Health, Education and Welfare, and earlier volumes of the Commission).

58. Harry I. Greenfield and O. W. Anderson, "The Medical Care Price Index," Research Series No. 7, Health Information Foundation New York, 1960, Chart III. It should be noted that the Consumer Price Index, of which the Medical Care Price Index is a component, measures prices only and not costs, though in the hospital field the correlation between the two is quite high.

59. Excellent versions of many of the reports cited may be found in Somers, op. cit., chap. 8, and Somers and Somers, Medicare and the Hospitals (Washington, D.C.: Brookings Institution, 1967), passim.

60. "The Size and Shape of the Medical Care Dollar," op. cit., p. 12, and New York Times, April 2, 1974.

61. New York Times, February 21, 1974.

62. Some recent examples of consumer critiques of health care are Heal Yourself, Report of the Citizens' Board of Inquiry Into Health Services For Americans (Washington, D. C.: American Public Health Association, 1972), and Donald K. Ross, A Public Citizen's Action Manual (New York: Grossman Publishers, 1973), chap. 2.

63. "Federal and State Legislation Requiring Participation in Health," Community Health Institute, New York, 1971.

64. New York Times, December 20, 1973.

65. Ibid.

66. See the interesting article by Walter J. McVerney, "Medicine Faces the Consumer Movement," Prism, September 1973.

CHAPTER

2

VETERANS
ADMINISTRATION
HOSPITALS

The not-for-profit sector of the health care field, as we have previously pointed out, is comprised of both voluntary and governmental units. Our task in the present chapter and in the one following is to explore the governmental part of the field, focusing on the federal level here and on state and county units in Chapter 3.

First, a brief discussion of the major differences between the voluntary and governmental units may be appropriate. In contrast to voluntary hospitals which are in the main autonomous entities, governmental hospitals are created by acts of Congress or of state and local legislatures as a means of providing health services directly to the public or to specific segments thereof. As a function of government, these hospitals, further, are totally funded by tax revenues and, generally, supplied with manpower through Civil Service procedures. Of necessity, there is centralized control over multiple units scattered across the nation as well as overseas. Taking the Veterans Administration alone, we are dealing with what has been described as "the single largest system in the hospital and associated medical fields."[1] However, the legislative requirements which place control in a given agency such as the Veterans Administration do not necessarily conflict with varying degrees of decentralization in the actual administration of specific hospitals.

Besides differing with voluntary hospitals on matters of organization, control, funding, and staffing, federal units—especially in Veterans Administration hospitals—also differ in target populations. Voluntary hospitals are theoretically available to all persons in a community, or even beyond a given community, whereas VA hospitals are available solely for use by veterans, their dependents, and beneficiaries; and within the veterans group, further distinctions are made between peacetime and wartime veterans and between veterans with and without service-connected disabilities. With respect to the latter group, a means test for the purpose of establishing priorities, constitutes an additional barrier to care in VA hospitals. Needless to say, VA hospitals are open to veterans, but veterans may also be treated in other facilities which, if warranted, may be reimbursed by VA; and many if not most veterans seek health care in nonveteran facilities—in effect, shedding their veterans' status for this purpose. As a consequence of such categorical recipients, the very important factor of case mix must be kept in mind when comparisons are attempted between VA and other types of hospitals. More specifically, VA hospitals lack pediatric, gynecological, and obstetric services.

As of 1972, federal hospitals constituted 6 percent of all U.S. hospitals, owned 26 percent of all beds, accounted for 5 percent of all admissions and 21 percent of all outpatient visits.[2] Since these data are influenced by such factors as the numbers of patients in military hospitals as a result of hostilities or other service-connected activity, it is important to view the constituent parts of the total:[3]

TABLE 2.1

Federal Hospitals, 1972

Service or Group	Number
Air Force	77
Army	47
Navy	35
Public Health Service	13
Veterans Administration	160
Federal (other)	1
Public Health Service	
Indian Service	49
Department of Justice	19
Total	401

Apart from specifically military installations (the first three), Veterans Administration hospitals constitute the single largest group in the federal category and the bulk of our subsequent discussion relates to them.

The major dimensions of Veterans Administration health activities are shown in Appendix B, Table B-1.* Both the range of activities shown in the table as well as their quantitative aspects are noteworthy—over one million patients treated and over eleven million medical visits (including dental) during fiscal 1973. All told,[4]

> The Veterans Administration's Medical Care System at the end of Fiscal Year 1973 was providing care in 169 hospitals, 206 outpatient clinics, 82 nursing homes and 18 domiciliaries. Veterans were also given care under VA auspices in non-VA hospitals and in community nursing homes. In addition, the VA authorized, on a fee-for-service basis, visits to non-VA physicians and dentists for outpatient treatment, and supported veterans under care in hospitals, domiciliaries, and nursing homes operated by 38 states.

INTERNAL ACCOUNTABILITY

Legal Accountability

The Veterans Administration was established as an "independent agency" under the President by an Executive Order in 1930—consolidating into one department several branches of government previously concerned with veterans' affairs.[5] Funds for the operation of the Veterans Administration are provided through Congressional appropriations, the major interested group being the House Committee on Veterans' Affairs. The Senate also maintains an interest through its Subcommittee on Veterans' Affairs of the Committee on Labor and Public Welfare. The Administrator of Veterans Affairs submits an annual report both to the President of the Senate as well as to the Speaker of the House of Representatives. The enabling Executive

---

*Discrepancies between the number of VA hospitals in 1972 shown in Table 1 above (160) and the number in the Appendix Table (169) are due either to definitional changes or to different reporting periods, or both—in any event, a matter which, for the present study, is not significant.

Order mentioned above might be considered the analog of the voluntary
hospital's charter, and the Congress may be viewed in part as comparable to the corporations' departments of the various States.

Governance Accountability

The Veterans Administration is headed by an Administrator of
Veterans Affairs who is appointed to the position by the President
with the advice and consent of the Senate. The agency (hereafter
the VA Central Office) is organized into three major departments
reporting directly to the Administrator. The department of interest
here is the Department of Medicine and Surgery, which in turn is
headed by a Chief Medical Director with various Assistant Chiefs
(for professional services, research and education, administration,
and the like) as subordinates. The lines of authority continue down-
ward to Regional Medical Directors, to whom the directors of the
individual VA hospitals, clinics, and domiciliary facilities report.
The salient difference in governance structure between the VA and
voluntary hospitals is the absence of a board of directors or trustees
from the former. Other things being equal, the omission of a governing board should make for a more sharply focused administration
with fewer intraorganizational conflicts. In fact, one VA hospital
administrator interviewed in connection with the present study remarked, "I constitute the governing body," and went on to say that
he preferred the added authority-cum-responsibility of a single-
headed administration to his prior "headaches" with the board of
trustees of a voluntary hospital.
      Still another way in which the VA administrator operates with
fewer constraints than his voluntary hospital counterpart is in his
dealings with unions. Nonprofessional employees in VA hospitals
are members of the American Federation of Government Employees;
therefore the major parameters of wages, hours, pensions and working
conditions are determined centrally in Washington in negotiations
between the Union and the Civil Service Commission, leaving relatively
minor administrative matters to be settled locally between the administrator and union representatives. The delimitation of managerial
perogatives occasioned by local militant unions, as in the voluntary
hospitals' case, does not exist in the VA situation.
      Worth noting too is the fact that since the VA hospitals are federal
institutions, many local and state regulations and ordinances which
apply to voluntaries do not apply to them. Reference here is to the
submission of various reports to city and state health and social
service departments. Nor until recently were VA hospitals required

to abide by decisions of local and state health planning councils on
such crucial matters as capital construction and on operating programs. * It turns out, therefore, that in place of the increased bureaucratic control one might expect from a government operation, the VA
administrator is in fact faced with fewer such constraints than is the
case in voluntary hospitals.

Interestingly, this relative lack of bureaucratic restraint extends,
as well, to the internal organization of the hospital. One author found,
for instance,[6] that

> . . . the degree of external control does not
> foster the buraucratization of professionals,
> contrary to what one might expect on the basis
> of stereotypes about governmental bureaucracies.
> The more "autonomous" voluntary hospitals tend
> to have the highest levels of bureaucratization
> while the "extremely controlled" VA hospitals
> have the lowest levels.

Another difference with respect to governance between voluntaries
and VA hospitals is that in the latter the medical staff functions without a separate set of bylaws or "constitution." Again, this reinforces
the unicapitate administrative structure mentioned earlier. As Roemer
and Friedman put it, "There are not two lines of authority—one medical
and the other administrative—which can clash."[7]

The foregoing statements do not imply that all internal governance
problems are obviated by a single-headed administrative structure.
Dr. Marc J. Musser, then Chief Medical Director of the VA's Department of Medicine and Surgery, reported some discontent on the part
of interns and residents of several VA hospitals who maintained that

---

*There has been an important policy change in this respect
recently. A Veterans Administration Planning and Evaluation letter
dated July 12, 1972, stated that, "Office of Management and Budget
directives have been revised to require that for certain construction
projects we [the VA] must obtain the Area-Wide and State Comprehensive Health Planning Council's approval prior to inclusion of such
projects in the annual budget submission. As such projects are
planned, we will specifically advise and assist in this new approach.
Our level of involvement with these councils may then directly affect
the outcome of our own proposals."

" . . . communications among house officers, the hospital directors and the VA staff in the Central Office were either nonexistent or in need of improvement."[8]

The correctives initiated by the VA Central Office included placing house staff physicians on major policy-making bodies and the creation of a new office of house staff affairs within the Central Office with two Public Health Service physicians acting as "ombudsmen for all VA house staff."[9]

Professional Accountability

Much if not all of what was previously mentioned with regard to professional self-image of physicians and other autonomous professionals within the voluntary system applies equally to the Veterans Administration hospital system. There are, however, at least two important differences to which attention should be drawn.

1. Since a far higher proportion of VA hospitals than voluntaries are affiliated with medical schools (the ratio currently exceeds 60 percent) the latter, more specifically, the "Dean's Committees" of the medical schools exercise an important influence over the selection of staff. Most if not all physicians appointed to VA hospitals have consequently been approved by medical schools.

2. Perhaps an even more important difference between VA and voluntary hospitals lies in the fact that a much greater proportion of the staff of VA institutions are full-time, salaried, or contractual physicians. As of 1972, close to 40 percent of the physicians were on full time status, a figure which approaches 90 percent if residents and interns are included.[10] Additionally, most of the part time physicians devote more than half of their time to the VA. As a result of the fact that so great a proportion of the staff receives income only from the hospital, "their sense of obligation to the hospital," say Roemer and Friedman, "is likely to be greater than that felt in a loosely structured MSO [Medical Staff Organization] by a private physician whose total funds and reward come from his patient."[11] The same authors also point out that the full-time payment system attracts physicians who can (and who prefer to) work within a team framework as contrasted with the private fee-for-services practitioner. While it is difficult to document, the salaried physician generally is presumed to increase his knowledge and abilities by virtue of the team situation; he is also likely to be more research-oriented and more concerned with the quality of care he renders. The VA physician is also accountable to the chiefs of service and to various Standard Boards within the hospital as well as to the Standard Board in Washington.

As indicated in Appendix Table A-2, a high proportion of federal hospitals have JCAH accreditation—which means they possess tissue, utilization review, and medical audit committees for internal maintenance of standards.

Internal Flow of Funds

Funds for the operation of the entire Veterans Administration system are initially requested by the President. * The initial request is then considered both by the Appropriations Committee of the House and by the Office of Management and Budget.

Administrators of individual VA hospitals are provided with an annual prospective budget based in part on the expected average patient-day census of the hospital, patient turnover rates, and anticipated outpatient load and capital needs.

When, as in the past, the budget allocations were based solely on average census, excess patient stays resulted. [12]

Heydebrand[13] pointed out in this connection that

> . . . average length of stay may be influenced by
> budgetary and administrative considerations totally
> extraneous to the medical decisions involved. Thus,
> a study of VA tuberculosis hospitals shows that dis-
> charge rates did not exceed a certain limit so as to
> maintain a certain average daily patient census and
> to prevent budgetary cuts.

Later in his book, however Heydebrand presents a somewhat contradictory view: "Federal VA hospitals rank low in de jure legal political autonomy, but high in de facto economic autonomy, since budgets are prepared on the basis of relatively high standards of patient care."[14] After the budget is prepared, the Administrator, as Klarman indicated, "has considerable discretion in spending his annual allotment. He is also held to a high degree of accountability after spending it."[15]

---

*In Fiscal Year 1974 the request totaled $12.2 billion, with 23 percent allocated to medical programs (HUD report, p. 478).

By no means the only measure of the efficiency with which the administrator has managed the funds under his disposal is provided by data on the cost per day of providing care. A (too small) comparison of the costs in VA and community hospitals reveals the following:[16]

Community Versus VA Hospital Costs per Diem

Calendar year 1969	$70.03	Fiscal year 1970	$38.42
Calendar year 1970	81.01	Fiscal year 1971	43.41
Calendar year 1971	92.31	Fiscal year 1972	52.87

The reader should recall here our earlier strictures regarding VA and non-VA comparisons. The ratio of VA costs to community hospital costs would yield a somewhat better measure, but the three observations do not provide an adequate basis for generalizing. In 1969 the VA/Community ratio was 55 percent; in 1970 it was 54 percent and in 1971, 57 percent. The fact that the absolute differences between the two sets of rates increased in each of the years, is, we would think, of some significance: the differentials being $31.61, $37.60 and $39.44. On a per case basis, however, VA costs exceed those of community hospitals due to the longer length of stays in the former—which again is a function of the case mix.

Financial accountability is also reinforced by fiscal audits of hospitals performed by the VA Central Headquarters. Such audits, "are scheduled at recurring intervals depending upon the quality evaluation of the previous audit, and are generally accomplished at intervals ranging from 18 to 35 months. During fiscal year 1973, fiscal audits were conducted at 46 hospitals. . . ."[17] In addition, "negotiated contracts are reviewed for adequacy of contract terms and validity of cost and pricing data. Audits are made on active contracts for services, such as hospital treatment, to assure cost data submitted are adequate and accurate to support payments."[18]

The administrator of a VA hospital is also required by law to submit an Annual Report of Position Reviews and Comparative Average Salaries and Grades as well as a Report (whenever violation occurs) of expenditure or obligation in excess of appropriations or apportionment as required by the Anti-Deficiency Act.[19]

Following is an excerpt of a letter sent to a VA hospital administrator by the Chief Medical Director of the VA after the Administrator himself notified the Chief of a violation:

PERSONAL-OFFICIAL

Mr. _____
Hospital Director
VA Hospital

Dear Mr. _____

Your letter of August 2, 1968, has been reviewed, and it has been
determined that a violation of the Anti-Deficiency Act occurred on
June 30, 1968, in Appropriation 3680160.

You as the Hospital Director are primarily responsible for the violation, under the general rule stated in paragraph 3A.03c(4), VA
Manual MP-4, Part V. Control was not exercised in a manner that
would have prevented the creation of obligations in excess of the
allotment available.

You have informed us that the system of administrative control of
funds is adequate. The proper exercise of the prescribed controls
will prevent any recurrence of a violation.

Sincerely yours,

_____
Chief Medical Director

It should be noted that the Chief Medical Director advised the
Administrator of Veterans Affairs who in turn notified the Director
of the Bureau of the Budget, the Speaker of the House and the President of this violation which involved the sum of $3,300. Few if any
hospital administrators in any other facilities in the United States
are subject to the same degree of fiscal accountability.

EXTERNAL ACCOUNTABILITY

Legal

Much of what was discussed above concerning internal legal,
governance, and fiscal accountability applies to external accountability as well, and need not be repeated here—the reason being
that VA hospitals, unlike voluntaries, are accountable to one source
(the Congress) for their charters and for the receipt and disposition
of funds.

The fact of government ownership introduces some new legal problems. As in all cases of governmental control, a patient in a VA hospital who wishes to bring suit against the hospital and/or a physician will first have to obtain the permission of the government in order to commence.

Governance

Not unlike the case of voluntaries, where administrators are appointed by a board, most officials and many subordinates are appointed by the VA Central Office, and of course they are responsible to that office. Lower-echelon personnel presumably obtain positions from competitive civil service lists. As a consequence, it may be more difficult for an administrator to discharge or to transfer personnel. This introduces some constraints on personnel management similar to those mentioned earlier, which are imposed on voluntary administrators by the existence of strong unions or professional associations.

Again, as in the case of many government agencies which operate locally but which are subject to ultimate—albeit remote—control from Washington, a considerable amount of buck passing may take place. This potential for shifting responsibility and accountability along with its inevitable accompaniment of red tape may reduce the effectiveness of the administrator as well as the system as a whole. Undoubtedly, a well-trained and experienced administrator who runs a tight ship can do much to minimize the potential for what might be termed "governance slippage."

Quality and Functional Accountability

The frequency and intensity of criticism of VA hospitals fluctuates with war and postwar periods. At such times VA hospitals are caught between a rapidly escalating demand for services and acute shortages of personnel. The critiques are all the more poignant, since many VA patients are para- and quadriplegics, or acute burn victims, or other such products of modern warfare. Moreover, many of the "exposes" of VA hospitals are undertaken by popular media for purposes other than those of finding solutions to the problems raised. Three of the more serious attempts to analyze the situation in VA hospitals are contained in the 1970 Hearings before the Subcommittee on Veterans' Affairs of the U.S. Senate (the Cranston Report); the HUD–Space-Science Veterans Appropriation Hearings before the House Committee on Appropriations in 1973, both of which have previously been noted; and a Nader report, Troubled Peace: An Epilogue to Vietnam. [20]

It is beyond the purview of the present work to present a detailed analysis of these reports or to evaluate them. Our particular concern is the degree to which the critiques (to the extent they are valid) are due to accountability problems of one sort or another. None of the reports cited addressed themselves directly to this problem.

For example, in his opening remarks Senator Alan Cranston (D., California), asserted that both Democrats and Republicans "share responsibility for whatever lack of funds for personnel and facilities faces us in this field," and further remarked, "nor can the Veterans Administration be singled out for blame. It has to make do with whatever the Congress and the Administration provide."[21] This, of course, is a problem in the accountability of Congress to the people, rather than a problem of accountability endemic to the VA per se.

The consequences of inadequate funding, however, fall most heavily on the individual VA hospital and result in drastic reductions of services, quality, and overall efficiency. As a case in point, the director of the Philadelphia VA hospital, in a memorandum dated January 15, 1970 to his Division and Service Chiefs, stated:[22]

> The hospital operating budget remains critically short in support of the Hospital's operational needs. Supplemental funding from our Central Office in Washington, D.C., in sufficient amounts to raise our deficits from the critical category, appears to be a distinct improbability.
>
> We, therefore, face a monumental task in reassessing our current objectives and curtailing our operations to an operating level consistent with our monetary support.
>
> I am asking you Division and Service Chiefs, as an integral part of our Hospital management team, each and everyone to fully accept your supportive role in obtaining our objectives in this crisis. Your resulting actions may cause unpleasantness, distaste and may appear to be undesirable and unsatisfactory, but I assure you that curtailment of sizable expenditures is most necessary.
>
> Consistently over the past several months, we have kept you informed that our monetary deficits were in excess of $600,000 for the current fiscal year. The situation remains the same.
>
> Certain distinct areas which come to mind where savings can be effected are in overtime, outside laboratory tests, reduced employment, reduced patient census and curtailment of supplies, equipment and services. You, as Division and Service Chiefs, will

undoubtedly have more specific ideas and plans. Please
feel free to contribute any facts or theories which come
to mind.

Effective immediately, overtime will be drastically
curtailed. Outside clinical laboratory tests will be reduced to those absolutely essential and must be approved
by the Service Chief as well as the Chief, Laboratory
Service. All other outside tests such as EEG's, et
cetera, must be approved by the Service Chief and the
Chief of Staff. Replacement of employees who separate
or transfer will require the approval of the Personnel
Control Board and will be on a highly selective basis.

Finally, may I ask your full support in carefully reviewing your service and division requests for supplies,
equipment and services.

The second-named hearings, HUD, contained a report by the
Surveys and Investigations Staff of the House Appropriations Committee
to the Chairman with respect to the "management of the medical care
programs of the Veterans Administration and implementation of work
load and patient care standards as specified in the Appropriations
Act."[23] The latter act required that the 1973 appropriations to the
VA provide no less than 98,500 operating beds, a minimum average
daily patient load of 85,500, and a minimum staff/patient ratio of
1.49 to 1 in all VA hospitals.[24] Precise stipulations such as these
are a prelude to trouble from three major sources: (1) the funds
provided will be inadequate due to rising (especially medical) costs;
(2) funds authorized may not be released by the Office of Management
and Budget; and (3) there is a failure to differentiate VA hospitals
by size, function, location, and patient mix.

The HUD investigative study was critical of the VA for not ad-
hering to the mandate, a criticism which was supported by the General
Accounting Office. Here the defense of the VA rested on the unwillingness of the Office of Management and Budget (OMB) to release funds
requested by the VA—shifting this to a question of OMB accountability
to Congress, and not one inherent in the VA.

Given the size and complexity of the VA hospital system, no
single evaluation of the level of quality can be possible or meaningful.
To illustrate some of the extremes:

1. The testimony of a second-year resident in medicine at the
Miami Veterans Administration Hospital recorded in the Cranston
report was an extremely critical one, concluding with his statement:
"I and the other ward physicians at the Miami Veterans Administration
Hospital cannot in good conscience continue to practice this quality
of medicine and offer this level of compromised medical care."[25]

2. On the other hand, Dr. Philip Lee, former Assistant Secretary for Health, Education, and Welfare, certified at the same hearings to the effect that " . . . the Veterans Administration has really pioneered in developing a system to assure quality and to monitor the quality of care provided," and quoted Dr. Roger O. Egeberg as stating, "I feel quite definitely that the Veterans Administration represents the top 20 percent of professional care and quality. . . ."[26]

3. The Nader Report's assessment of the overall quality of Veterans Administration Hospitals falls between the two stands. The report's authors felt that some of the above mentioned exposes were "too harsh because many community hospitals, in the inner city and rural areas, provide a much lower quality of care than the VA."[27] And in a statement which appears to go beyond the quality issue to broader aspects, the authors wrote, "In many ways, the VA hospital system, simply because it is a system, is less inefficient than most community hospitals, which operate as independent fiefdoms without the benefits of any coordination or system of accountability."[28]

The VA has recently instituted its own in-house version of the JCAH accreditation survey:[29]

> In FY1973 a procedure for evaluating the quality
> of medical care (known as district evaluation) was
> pre-tested in eight VA hospitals. Members of
> visiting evaluation teams evaluated both structural
> (management) and process (professional care)
> aspects of patient care, recording their objec-
> tions on standardized forms. Patient satisfac-
> tion with the care they received was measured
> by self-administered questionnaires. The data
> collected are being analyzed and consideration
> is being given to extending the district evalua-
> tion procedures to the total VA system.

The success of this program as a quality monitoring effort depends on the composition of the evaluating teams, the nature of the questionnaire, the randomness of patient selection, and finally the degree to which the feedback is utilized to effect indicated changes. It is too early to assess this aspect of VA quality control, but it is an attempt that bears watching.

Fiscal and Cost Accountability

Little need be added at this point to our earlier discussion concerning internal and external fiscal accountability. Perhaps the only additional point that should be stressed here—and it is one of great

importance so far as external fiscal accountability is concerned—is
the fact that, for all practical purposes, VA cost figures are available
not only to Congressional Committees and to the General Accounting
Office, but to the public as well. [30] This degree of disclosure of
operational and cost data does not occur in any other sector of the
health field and is a necessary (but not sufficient) condition for full
accountability. Additional aspects of the movement for full financial
disclosure are discussed in Chapter 6.

                        Interorganizational Accountability

    Our discussion of voluntary hospitals in Chapter 1 omitted refer-
ence to interorganizational accountability for the reason that autonomous
units are under no legal compulsion to cooperate one with the other.
Here and there one can find evidence of institutional cooperation on
the part of voluntary hospitals but the number of instances, in view
of the large potential, is miniscule. [31] One of the advantages of
government control is that one can accomplish by legislative fiat what
does not normally occur, or that which takes too long to transpire in
the private sector.
    Recognizing that the VA hospital was, in the words of Marc J.
Musser, its former Chief Medical Doctor, " . . . too long isolated
emotionally, professionally and organizationally from the private
and voluntary sector. . . ." Congress in 1966 passed Public Law
89-785 which "has proved to be one of the most far-reaching laws
ever enacted affecting the VA system in terms of bringing together
the community and the VA facilities. Called the 'sharing law,' it
permits and encourages the sharing of limited medical resources
between the VA facilities and those of the private sector and obviates
the duplication of expensive services and equipment." [32] Not only
does this law encourage interfacility cooperation among VA hospitals
themselves and between the VA and other governmental units (such as
Department of Defense and Public Health Service) but, most impor-
tantly, it is one of the few laudatory examples of intersectoral (public-
private) cooperation.
    The "sharing law" requires the Administration of Veterans Affairs
to prepare an Annual Report on Sharing Medical Facilities which lists
all of the parties to the sharing agreements, the medical resources
shared, the commencement dates and termination dates, if any. The
law has now been in effect for seven years and the number of agreements under it have grown. The 1973 Annual Report of the VA states
that "during FY 1973, there were 67 VA hospitals with approved

sharing agreements involving some 120 individual contracts. The services provided for in the contracts have an annual value of 4.5 million dollars."[33]

While the last few years have seen some noteworthy legislation developed to foster interinstitutional cooperation such as the Comprehensive Health Plan Act and the Regional Medical Programs, private-sector health facilities have not yet reached the stage attained by the VA in this area.

Consumer Accountability

Our veteran population is approaching 28 million and, counting families of veterans, the potential patients of the VA system approach 50 percent of the population—by far the largest potential consumer group of any health system in the country. The nature of the recipient group presents certain problems. Veterans have been eligible for care from the present VA health system for a quarter of a century. The bulk of the current veteran population consists of World War II veterans and it is this group which perforce controls most of the veterans' organizations, such as the American Legion and the Veterans of Foreign Wars. Furthermore, the World War II veterans are now in the middle and upper age brackets, so that their demands for care are based on chronic illnesses or on the need for nursing home or domiciliary care. The Nader group pointed out that "as the system has evolved, it has become heavily oriented toward long institutionalization and the care of chronic illness."[34] Korean and Vietnam veterans, on the other hand, are younger and require acute care or outpatient facilities, not to mention the severe spinal cord conditions, drug addiction, and other psychiatric disorders arising from the Vietnam conflict. It is to be expected therefore that in the interim period between accommodation of the VA health care system to World War II veterans and its adaptation to the veterans of the more recent conflicts, that intergenerational friction would develop.

A long-standing complaint against the VA stems from veterans with nonservice-connected illness. To quote from the Nader report, "The inability of the VA to treat nonservice-connected cases on an outpatient basis has historically been one of the most pernicious influences on the system."[35] The nonservice problem can easily be solved by legislative relief, but this would entail the allocation of vast additional funds for the system—again rendering this an accountability problem of the Congress to the people. Another problem which has assumed large proportions since the Vietnam conflict is the question of treating veterans with less-than-honorable discharges. Here again new legislative guidelines are required for some kind of solution, although these may be difficult to devise in view of the political questions and of the consequences for military discipline.

Since VA hospitals by definition are not community hospitals, and since they have a categorically defined population, the consumer movement in health has not touched them to any significant degree. This does not mean, however, that the VA is impervious to the winds of consumerism. Dr. Musser, an able spokesman for the system, has summed up the VA position as follows:[36]

> Much has been written about consumer participation in health care affairs. It might be said that the Veterans Administration has dealt longer with so-called consumer involvement than any other major health care organization. Daily, for 25 years, we have related to service organizations, civic groups and their representatives in the Congress. Whatever one's emotional bias might be their groups are consumers and are well enough informed so as to have asserted a considerable controlling influence. Their interests extend all the way from administration through quality of care, cost control, and the ultimate socio-economic predicament of the patient. With 4 million veterans in this country—who with their families constitute 40 percent of our population—we do not want for consumer reaction or involvement.

In attempting to rebut Ralph Nader's criticism of the VA as a relatively unscrutinized agency, Donald E. Johnson replied[37] that

> "At least four major committees of Congress constantly study our operations, and at one time or another some 19 Congressional Committees have scrutinized facets of VA operations. The great medical schools of the nation review VA medical operations on a daily basis and veterans organizations offer constant and often critical evaluations of VA's performance.

As an ironic postscript, we should point out that Donald Johnson resigned as Administrator of Veteran Affairs in May 1974. Included among the many charges made against his administration by Congressional and Veterans' groups was one of poor medical care at VA hospitals. [38] Undoubtedly the readjustment problems of VA hospitals to the needs of the younger veterans—especially in the cases of drug[39] and psychiatric problems and of rehabilitation—were very real, but, in our view, the VA hospitals have the basic resources (capability and motivation) to deal with these areas; the remedies here are time and money. The really telling accusations concerned involuntary political contributions exacted by high officials for the Nixon re-election campaign, improper hiring of politicians, and general managerial inefficiency. The VA hospitals administration was not charged with these abuses. One might speculate that its professional mission and orientation served to insulate the Department of Medicine and Surgery to some degree from the political machinations of the bureaucracy at the top.

CONCLUSION

Unlike the case of voluntary hospitals, which are in the main subject to 50 different state administrations, VA and other federal hospitals have the advantage of centralized control. Criticisms of quality of care or of any other medical aspects of VA hospitals are focused into the VA Central Agency and responses and remedies can flow directly from the center to each of the individual units. Moreover, since federal hospitals must rely on appropriations from Congress, that body must assume a share of the burden for whatever deficiencies in care exist that may be traceable to inadequate funding.

As we have indicated, there are many effective avenues of external accountability in federal hospitals; major problems still exist, however, in the areas of internal accountability. For a variety of reasons VA hospitals have not attained the prestige status of the large voluntary hospitals, and since the most qualified physicians are attracted by (as well as they help to determine) prestige, internal standards of professional accountability may as a result be diminished.

Traditional attitudes of professional medical organizations towards government control and operation of health facilities undoubtedly still play a role in the inability to attract many physicians. The gradual extension of government "intervention" in voluntary hospitals occasioned by Titles 18 and 19 have, however, tended to narrow the regulatory gap and national health insurance will narrow it still further. The consequence of these trends is that VA hospitals may gain a relative attractiveness and the internal problems to which we referred will become fewer. For the longer run, the economies of scale and the efficiencies of centralized administration inherent in federal operation, will be the factors many health planners will study as they contemplate reconstruction of the health care delivery system.

NOTES

1. "Operations of Veterans' Administration Hospital and Medical Program," Committee on Veterans' Affairs, House Committee Print No. 9, 93rd. Cong., 1st Sess., Washington, D.C. 1973, p. 1.

2. See Appendix A, Table A-1.

3. Personal communication to author from American Hospital Association, May 6, 1974.

4. Administrator of Veterans Affairs, Annual Report, 1973, Washington, D.C., p. 9.

5. United States Government Manual, Office of the Federal Register (formerly U.S. Government Organization Manual), Washington D.C., p. 575.

6. Wolf V. Heydebrand, Hospital Bureaucracy: A Comparative Study of Organizations (New York: Dunellen Publishing Co., 1973), p. 223.

7. Milton I. Roemer and Jay W. Friedman, Doctors in Hospitals (Baltimore: Johns Hopkins Press, 1971), p. 200.

8. Marc J. Musser, "VA Regionalization Fears Prove False," U.S. Medicine, January 15, 1972, p. 12.

9. Ibid.

10. "Operations of Veterans . . . " op. cit., p. 14.

11. Roemer and Friedman, op. cit., p. 198.

12. "HUD-Space-Science-Veterans Appropriations for 1974," Hearings Before the Subcommittee of the Committee on Appropriations, House of Representatives, 93rd Cong., 1st Sess., Washington, D.C., 1973, p. 514.

13. Heydebrand, op. cit., p. 62.

14. Ibid., p. 287.

15. Herbert E. Klarman, Hospital Care in New York City (New York: Columbia University Press, 1963), p. 283.

16. "HUD-Space-Science-Veterans Appropriations," op. cit., p. 16.

17. Administrator of Veterans Affairs, op. cit., p. 97.

18. Ibid.

19. Communication to the author from the Office of the Controller, Veterans Administration; see Appendix B-2.

20. Paul Starr, Jim Henry, and Ray Bonner, Troubled Peace: An Epilogue to Vietnam, the Nader Report on Vietnam Veterans and the Veterans Administration (Washington, D.C.: Center for Study of Responsive Law, 1973), preliminary draft, chap. 4-5.

21. Oversight of Medical Care of Veterans Wounded in Vietnam, Hearings Before the Subcommittee on Veterans Affairs, 91st. Cong., 1st and 2nd Sess., November 1969—January 1970, Washington, D.C., p. 3.

22. Ibid., p. 516.

23. "HUD-Space-Science-Veterans Appropriations," op. cit., p. 1162.

24. Ibid., p. 1166.

25. Oversight of Medical Care . . . , op. cit., p. 484.

26. Ibid., p. 198.

27. Starr et al., op. cit., pp. iv-v.

28. Ibid., pp. iv-v.

29. Administrator of Veterans Affairs, op. cit., p. 59.

30. Ibid., pp. 53-54, 149 and Table 33, "Cost of Operation of Medical Inpatient Facilities—Fiscal Year 1973."

31. "Combinations and Mergers," American College of Hospital Administration, Chicago, 1970. See also Mark S. Blumberg, Shared Services for Hospitals (Chicago: American Hospital Association, 1966).

32. Marc J. Musser, "Status of the Health Care System of the Veterans Administration's Department of Medicine and Surgery," Military Medicine 136, no. 10 (October 1971), pp. 788-789.

33. Administrator of Veterans Affairs, op. cit., p. 61.

34. Starr et al., op. cit., pp. iv-x.

35. Ibid., pp. vi.

36. Marc J. Musser and Benjamin B. Wells, "Shapes of the Future of the Health Care System As Seen from the Perspective of the Department of Medicine and Surgery of the Veterans Administration," January 20, 1971 (mimeo). (Emphasis in original.)

37. "HUD-Space-Science-Veterans Appropriations," op. cit., p. 642.

38. "Why The Vets Are Up in Arms," Newsweek, May 6, 1974.

39. See "Veterans Still Fighting Vietnam Drug Habits," New York Times Magazine, June 2, 1974.

CHAPTER

3

STATE AND LOCAL
HEALTH FACILITIES

The present discussion of health facilities owned by units of local and state governments completes the overview of publicly owned facilities begun in the preceding chapter.

What kinds of health facilities are, in fact, owned and operated by other-than-federal governmental units? The data in Appendix Tables A-1 and C-1 enable us to develop a quantitative and functional profile of state and local hospitals. From Table A-1 we note a little appreciated but most important statistic, namely, that state and local hospitals showed the greatest percentage increase of all of the control types over the last quarter of a century.[1] In terms of number of beds, state and locals also ranked high—second to voluntaries; they also registered first in admissions growth and were quite high in outpatient visits. Whereas federal governmental units showed decreases in hospitals and beds, state and local units, by contrast, showed strong growth trends. Clearly the growth of the public sector in hospitals is confined to its state and local segments. State and local units also increased in relative terms over the 1946-72 period; their relative shares grew in percent of all hospitals (now ranked second to voluntaries, as opposed to third in 1946), and as a percent of all beds and of admissions. It is only in the outpatient visits category where their relative position remained unchanged (in this case over a ten-year period).

Functionally, as is shown by the data in Appendix Table C-1, the following characteristics emerge:

(a) Local governmental units (city and county) ranked second in importance to voluntary hospitals in the short-term general hospital category—state units are relatively unimportant here.

48

(b) In the case of short-term psychiatric facilities, the dominance of proprietary hospitals is noteworthy. State units ranked third after voluntaries, and local units were not significant.

(c) Local and state units were not significant in the case of short-term specialty hospitals.

(d) When we examined long-term facilities (where the stays exceed 30 days), the public sector accounts for 95 percent of all beds in long-term general hospitals, with the federal units first and local and state units following in that order.

(e) The state government is predominant in the next category—long-term psychiatric, with 69 percent of all hospitals, and an even more significant 88 percent of all beds. Local units are of little consequence here.

(f) State units also rank first in the case of long-term tuberculosis and other respitory disease facilities, with local units second.

(g) In the long-term specialty category, local units are important, ranking under the voluntaries; state units are also well represented with 19 percent of hospital and 25 percent of beds. [2]

In sum, these data show that state and local units are dominant in long-term facility types, whereas voluntary hospitals are mostly concerned with short-term stays (and hence disease types). Speculating on the reasons for this dichotomy we may postulate, first, that it would be very difficult for voluntary hospitals to operate on any viable financial basis where (to cite the definition) the "average length of stay for all patients is 30 days or more, or over 50 percent of all patients are admitted to units where average length of stay is 30 days or more." [3] An important part of the income of voluntary hospitals derives from the use of ancillary services provided to patients in the first few days of hospitalization; low patient turnover would obviously reduce these amounts. Second, long-term patients with chronic psychiatric illnesses or geriatric patients are not "interesting" to most physicians, especially to those in teaching hospitals. Third, extensive hospital stays soon exhaust the assets of most families, placing the patients in the medically indigent and, in short order, into the indigent categories.

Additional factors may also be cited. In the past at least, long-term psychiatric hospitals tended to be very large, making it difficult to secure enough low-cost land on which to build in urban centers, thereby shifting the problem to state authorities. The nature of the illnesses treated in long-term facilities—in the case of tuberculosis, highly communicable, and in the case of psychiatric illnesses, offensive to some societal tastes—are also factors which would lead to the assumption of these responsibilities by state governments in facilities distant from urban centers. The need for families of patients to have some degree of access to patients probably precluded federal activity in these areas.

INTERNAL ACCOUNTABILITY

Legal

Health facilities of state and local governments have their origins in and owe their continued existence to state legislatures, to boards of supervisors in the case of counties, or to city councils in the case of minicipal institutions. Each facility, in order to commence operations and to remain in service, must obtain an operating certificate—usually from the Departments of Health of the state or locality. (The latter requirements hold also for nongovernmental facilities.) Funds for capital construction as well as for operating purposes are voted by Ways and Means Committees, usually after approvals are given by special health subcommittees of the legislative bodies concerned. Most personnel are governed by rules of civil service.

Governance

Administrators of state and local health facilities are appointed by governors, mayors, city managers, or supervisory boards, generally from established civil service lists. (The practice is growing recently in New York municipal hospitals to set up "search committees," comprised of representatives of the Health and Hospitals Corporation, consumer advisory boards, and others, to fill vacancies or to staff new units outside of normal civil service procedures.) Individual administrators are accountable then directly to the health commissioners who in turn are accountable to the governors and legislatures.

Again, as for federal units, there are no boards of trustees in state and local institutions. In the absence of any information to the contrary, the same assumptions we made concerning single-headed administrations in Veterans Administration hospitals would appear to apply to state and local facilities as well. The similarities go even further. Just as the house staff of VA hospitals (as noted above) complained about their lack of input, so the house staff (interns and residents) complained about their lack of involvement in the "decision making" process in New York City's municipal hospitals.[4]

While most of the nonprofessional workers are civil servants, they do belong to unions. In New York State, for example, the state, county, and municipal workers' union covers most of the employees, and there are other civil service associations as well, such as the Civil Service Employees Association.

As in VA (and indeed any other hospitals), the M. D. Chiefs of Service exercise a great deal of influence and may be said to constitute a second main power center, taking the form usually of a Medical Board or of an Executive Committee of the various services.

Professional Accountability

The history of professional accountability in the case of state and local health facilities may be traced to the origins of public involvement in health care. A citation from the Piel Commission's report on New York City is informative:[5]

> Hospitals were first opened to the poor; the well-off could afford to be sick at home. In creating the municipal hospital system more than 150 years ago to take care of the "emergent and indigent sick," the City made this service a function and obligation of government. As voluntary hospitals grew up alongside the municipal system, the City continued to carry the main burden of care for the medically indigent. More important, although the charters of the private, non-profit voluntary hospitals require them to render care to any person who comes to their doors, these hospitals exercise selectivity, to a greater or lesser degree, in admitting patients. The City hospitals remain the sure, if last, resort.

While admittedly few other cities in the United States are as heavily involved in hospital care as is New York, the difference is one of degree, not kind. Local and state units were established mainly for the purpose of indigent care, giving rise to the term "dual care"— one for the poor and the other for paying patients. Inevitably, as the cliche has it, medicine for the poor becomes poor medicine.

A combination of circumstances in New York City, but undoubtedly replicated in part elsewhere, led inexorably to a crisis: rising costs of hospital care, competition with other health facilities for scarce resources, fragmented lines of authority, inadequate funds for maintenance and modernization. As a consequence of these major problems, city hospitals generally "failed to attract the house staff of qualified

residents and interns who traditionally render most of the care to
ward patients in voluntary and public hospitals."[6] As the Piel Commission's Final Report explained,[7]

> Residents and interns with questionable qualifications
> from medical schools overseas came in to supply the
> overwhelming majority of house staffs in the city
> hospitals. In the absence of adequate supervison
> by qualified seniors, these residents and interns
> were generally short-changed for the services they
> rendered at shamefully low compensation. Many of
> these house officers could not speak English and so
> worked in almost total isolation from any meaningful
> contact with most of their patients, as well as from
> the local medical community. City hospitals pro-
> ceeded to lose what standing they had as teaching
> institutions, and patient care in these hospitals
> depreciated correspondingly.

Similar allegations concerning the numbers of unlicensed physicians
in state owned facilities have also been made. For example, Dr.
Robert L. Taylor, a psychiatrist with the Community Mental Health
Services in Marin County, California, stated that in New York and
Ohio "40 percent of the physicians in the state mental hospitals are
unlicensed."[8]

The major attempt to change the course of professional deteriora-
tion in New York's municipal hospitals was through the mechanism of
affiliation contracts. Under a new policy instituted by the Commissioner
of Hospitals in 1961, New York City contracted with "selected teaching
and strong voluntary hospitals to staff specific municipal hospitals with
medical and technical personnel under budgetary terms covering
salaries, a percentage of overhead, and some equipment and supply
purchasing capability."[9]

It is generally agreed that the affiliation procedure, though not
an unqualified success, had positive effects on the municipal hospital
system. Among the improvements noted were an upgrading in the
quality of the medical staff, an improvement in recruiting better house
staff, and the training and supervision of the house staff by the affiliated
institution.[10]

With regard, more specifically, to professional accountability
questions, the report just cited contained a critique by the Health
and Hospitals Corporation (a new public-benefit corporation created
in 1970 to supervise the municipal hospitals) of inadequate recordkeeping, including physician failure to complete medical charts, and
failure to complete physician's certification and recertification forms

(certifying the patients' continuing need for medical treatment and hospital care), as well as laxity of utilization review committees.[11] Whether these managerial deficiencies are attributable to the combination of municipal ownership and superagency control is an extremely important but still debatable question.

Not having a comparable survey of state-owned facilities, our guess is that the problems of professional accountability noted above are compounded, due in the first instance to inadequate funding, and secondly, to the general scarcity of psychiatric and rehabilitation manpower.[12]

Internal Flow of Funds

By the terms of the enabling legislation which establishes local and state governmental health facilities, annual financial reports are customarily mandated. Such reports are subject to audit by comptrollers offices of cities and states, as well as by interested committees of the respective legislatures in much the same fashion as the Veterans Administration hospitals discussed previously. Two nagging questions may be raised here. One is the extent to which poor recordkeeping and the lack of bookkeeping and accounting personnel diminishes the accuracy of the financial reporting. The second is the disincentive to the use of stringent financial controls arising from the fact that excesses of revenue over costs do not remain with the individual facility but are required to be turned over to state or local governmental treasuries.

EXTERNAL ACCOUNTABILITY

Legal Accountability

Legal recourse in the case of state and local units is complicated by the fact (already noted above in the Veterans Administration case) that individuals must obtain permission to sue from the jurisdictions in question. Additionally, some very acute legal questions arise because state units are primarily psychiatric. The difficult problems arising from voluntary or involuntary incarceration and from discharges to home or to "halfway houses" of mental patients have given rise to acrimonious debate between psychiatrists on the one hand and civil liberties lawyers on the other.[13]

Governance

What was said in the previous chapter regarding internal governance in the VA case applies, mutatis mutandis, to state and local
units. Klarman[14] points out, with respect to New York City Municipal
Hospitals, that "there is a greater than normal separation of authority
and responsibility for expenditures and personnel in municipal hospitals, with authority lodged chiefly in the office of the Bureau of the
Budget."
One of the aims of the Health and Hospitals Corporation was, in
fact, to draw authority and responsibility together by a process of
decentralization under which each separate facility would have greater
authority with respect to budget preparation and allocation of funds.
In the New York City municipals, the administrators are responsible
for submitting annual reports: the reports are forwarded to the Health
and Hospital Corporation, where they are included in one Annual
Report, which is then sent to the Mayor. For state-owned facilities,
the reports are submitted to the Department of Health or to the Department of Mental Hygiene and the consolidated Departmental Annual
Reports are sent to the Governor and to the state legislature.

Quality and Functional Accountability

In 1972 the Council of Urban Health Providers, together with the
Health Services and Mental Health Administration, undertook an assess
ment of public hospitals (emphasis being placed primarily on city
and county institutions). [15] Among the positive aspects noted by the
participants in five regional conferences were the following:

1.   The public hospital "is the major provider of inpatient and am-
     bulatory care to the cities' poor and minority groups."
2.   "The public hospital provides quality, expensive services in
     specialized areas such as emergency services, kidney centers,
     burn centers and alcohol and drug detoxification. These are
     responsibilities which many private hospitals do not or will not
     assume.
3.   Public hospitals, "are . . . the major training ground for our
     nation's health manpower."

Among the major negative aspects noted were

1.   Obsolete physical plants.
2.   Difficult access due to a single central location.

3.   Long waits in outpatient and admitting services.
4.   "Some budget and civil service constraints [which] often inhibit
     the assembly of top-quality staff and often result in ineffective
     management.[16]

The four negatives (and many more) noted above were amply
documented in the case of New York's municipal hospitals in the Piel[17]
and Burlage reports.[18] Further corroboration of the critiques was
provided in the study of physicians' perceptions also noted above.[19]
A highly critical study of the public hospitals in Los Angeles contained
many of the previous points, and included the following long-standing
critique:[20]

> Dumping of patients on the public hospital by other com-
> munity hospitals is (another) critical problem. Already
> overburdened, the public hospital must take in these
> patients who are unwanted elsewhere, who show up in
> ambulances, unannounced, often without proper medical
> records. They come in "dead or nearly dead," according
> to one doctor in Washington. This happens to the tune of
> 1,300 patients a month in Los Angeles. These patients
> are often considered simply "undesirable" by the trans-
> ferring hospital, for reasons of their conditions, such
> as alcoholics going into DTs, or for reasons of race or
> poverty. The decision to transfer, or to dump, is fre-
> quently a snap judgment, not even made by a physician.

Roemer and Friedman, commenting on the relationship between
municipal and voluntary hospitals, point out that "in a large city . . .
the availability of a highly organized out-patient service at a municipal
hospital . . . reduces the pressure on nearby voluntary hospitals to
develop such programs."[21] Brecher and Ostow noted that "the changing
demographic patterns, the declining number of physicians in poorer
neighborhoods, and inadequate financing for alternative services,
which account for the unplanned growth of emergency rooms, also
explains the increasing load on the OPDs of the city hospitals."[22]
     It is axiomatic among hospital administrators that it is in the
outpatient clinics and in the emergency rooms where the largest
financial deficits arise. The data in Appendix C show the most recent
distribution of emergency room and outpatient visits for New York
City.
     The disproportionate share of municipals is clearly evident—with
13 percent of all hospitals and 27 percent of all beds in New York
City, they account for 51 percent of all emergency visits and 49 percent of all outpatient visits. Predictably, the proprietaries, with

6 percent of hospitals, account for only 2 percent of all emergency
visits and no outpatient visits whatever.

Using hospital approvals and affiliations as an objective approach
to the assessment of quality, Table B-1 indicates that state and local
facilities have below average rates of accreditation by the Joint
Commission on Accreditation of Hospitals (57 percent as opposed to
72 percent for all hospitals); they are also below average in other
types of accreditation, although they exceed the averages for Blue
Cross and Medicare certification.

Medicare and Medicaid certification raise an interesting point
here. One writer pointed out that due to these federal financing
mechanisms, " . . . within a short period of time the concept of
full reimbursement will eliminate the old basis for providing different
facilities for indigent and paying patients."[23] In fact, some writers
went further and felt that "the advent of Medicaid and Medicare would
signal the end of public hospitals because people who had been using
them could now afford to pay for care in private institutions."[24]
Among the reasons cited by Ms. Tetelman for the continued viability
of public hospitals were[25]

    (a)   The public hospital is regarded as a community
           resource and the voluntary hospitals have clearly
           indicated that they are generally not interested in
           the typical public hospital patient.

    (b)   Complex regulations and procedures for payment
           drive the former patient back to the public hos-
           pital.

    (c)   Medicaid cutbacks by states.

A fourth reason for the continued existence of public hospitals
" . . . is that the public hospitals are constantly being given new
responsibilities which others are unwilling or unable to take on."[26]
Some of the new functions mentioned were the rehabilitation of
prisoners, the care of inmates of halfway houses, custodial facilities,
and, as mentioned earlier, mental hospitals which require medical
services of one sort or another.

Nevertheless, there are grounds for believing in a convergence
movement as between public (nonpsychiatric) and voluntary hospitals.
For one thing, there has been a radical transformation in the financial
statements of public hospitals so that currently they are increasingly
coming to resemble those of voluntary hospitals. To illustrate:
whereas Klarman indicated that private payments to New York City
municipal hospitals comprised 6.4 percent of total revenue sources
in 1957, a glance at the most recent report of the Health and Hospitals
Corporation shows that payments by Medicare ($73.4 million), plus

Medicaid ($280.0 million), plus Blue Cross (27.8 million), plus Self-Pay and (other) Third Parties ($19.8 million) now constitute more than 55 percent of all revenues and, conversely, whereas New York City tax funds made up more than 93 percent of all revenues in the earlier year, currently this item has decreased to about 40 percent. [27]

Not reflected in financial statements, but of equal importance to the convergence theory (at least for New York State) is the fact that all health facilities in New York State (with the exception of federal hospitals and mental institutions) are encompassed by the far-reaching provisions of Article 28 of the New York State Public Health law. * Public as well as private hospitals are now (since 1965) subject to identical treatment with respect to inspection, audit, facility construction and the like.

The New York State Department of Mental Hygiene, in an effort to improve the quality of care at state-operated mental retardation facilities, established "review committees" at all state schools (as distinct from state hospitals). The function of these committees is to evaluate, "each school's physical facilities and programs for compliance with nationally recognized accreditation standards developed by the Accreditation Council for Residential Facilities for the Mentally Retarded." [28] All the states now have received broad powers of supervision over health facilities under the provisions of Titles 18 and 19 (Medicare and Medicaid). As Anne Somers quite rightly indicated, federal intervention in financing has resulted in a strengthening of states' roles in regulation. [29]

Fiscal and Cost Accountability

Since, by definition, state and local health facilities are established and owned by the jurisdictions in question, public funds, either through the budgetary process or via general or special bond monies, are continuously flowing into these facilities. The amount of tax or other monies allocated to public facilities varies greatly, depending on the size and type of hospital in question. Earlier we pointed out that since the advent of Medicare and Medicaid the state and local share of

---

*Because of its great importance for New York and because it is being used as a model for other states, a description of Article 28 is included as an Appendix to this chapter—Appendix C-1.

annual expenses is decreasing and the federal share is increasing.
As in the case of the Veterans Administration hospitals described in
Chapter 2, annual budgets of health facilities are scrutinized with
some varying degrees of care by legislative committees responsible
for general budget questions, and by subcommittees with a special
interest in health. Further, since Medicare, Medicaid, Blue Cross
and other insured monies are now flowing into state and local hospitals,
financial supervision by insurance Commissioners and by state departments concerned with reimbursement and rate setting have been added.

New York State is one of a very few in the country which enacted
a Cost Control Law (1969) designed to monitor and to inhibit escalating
health care costs and all states were included in the Economic Stabilization program, a general anti-inflationary weapon that covered
health along with other costs. Capital construction funds have been
subject to review under the Hill-Burton legislation, and more recently
by the Comprehensive Health Planning and Public Health Services Act
of 1966.

In New York State and increasingly in other states, uniformity in
financial reporting has become a reality after many years of effort.
All health facilities in New York are required to submit to the Division
of Health Economics of the Health Department an Annual Report containing general and statistical information and a Uniform Financial
Report—a 31-page detailed document on all of the financial aspects
of the facility's operations. The latter report must be certified by
an independent public accountant. Moreover, as of 1974, the Uniform
Financial Report—and indeed every report to a state agency—will,
under new New York State legislation, become a public record subject
to complete disclosure. The same type of legislation was enacted
earlier in the California Hospital Disclosure Act of 1972.

Despite all of the innovations in the area of fiscal and cost
accountability, and of the broad new powers given the New York
State Department of Health, a recent Commission Report found many
areas to criticize. [30] Referring specifically to the Uniform Financial
Report, the Commission pointed out that "Hospitals are not required
to keep their books according to a uniform system of accounting. As
a result," the report continues, "one hospital may allocate the cost
of the orderly who carries an X-ray plate from the X-ray room to
the developing lab as part of the cost of producing the X-ray, while
another may allocate the cost to nursing costs. Thus, rigorously
valid comparisons cannot be made from one facility to another."[31]
If true, this critique is an extremely serious one but not quite as
fundamental as not reporting the X-ray procedure at all, or recording
it twice—which is possible under less rigorous and ad hoc reporting
systems. Once the overall reporting framework is established, specific
problems of internal cost allocation not only will become more visible
but will be easier to resolve.

Interfacility Programs

Although there is a reference, in the 1972 report of the New
York State Department of Mental Hygiene, [32] to the fact that several
programs involving the sharing of resources between state hospitals
and local community mental health agencies had been established,
there is no evidence that such programs are mandated or that they
are extensive—unlike the VA case noted in the prior chapter. There
was no reference to interfacility sharing in the 1972 Annual Report
of the New York State Department of Health. This is not, however,
an inference of a complete absence of such activities. [33] The same
applies to the most recent Annual Report of the New York City Health
and Hospitals Corporation. [34] If the New York observations apply
nationally, a gap in local and state health facility operation is exposed—
one that, it would seem, should be closed, if quality and cost questions
are to be more adequately addressed.

Consumer Accountability

The Temporary State Commission, whose report was cited above,
made the following points with regard to the role of the consumer:[35]

> The Commission has found that information relating
> to health care services and having direct impact on the
> cost and quality of the services received by the residents
> of New York State is unavailable to consumers and others
> who need it; and that one of the most essential require-
> ments for the improvement of health services is a better
> informed and participating public;
> The Commission has found that the health care con-
> sumer and the health insurance subscriber have been
> almost totally eliminated from effective participation in
> decisions regarding treated service costs, expenditures
> or availability.

These are rather general statements, and no particular types
of facilities were singled out as cases in point. Of the three New
York reports cited earlier, only that of the New York City Health
and Hospitals Corporation made specific mention of consumer input.
The report noted that "community boards" had been set up in 17 of
the 19 municipal facilities with the last two in process. The boards
"contained a majority of members who depend upon the institutions
for their primary source of treated care services," and participate

in both capital and expense budget preparations," making this the
"first time that individual hospital communities had played an active
role in the budget-making process."[36]

The conference on public hospitals cited above also produced
some hortatory statements concerning "a greater role for the consumer
in determining the care he receives in a public institution."[37]

Just as the American Legion and similar organizations act as
interest groups of patients in VA hospitals, so organizations such as
the New York State Associaton for Retarded Children act as general
lobbying groups for residents in state psychiatric facilities. As a
result of the adverse publicity generated by the Willowbrook State
School expose, the Benevolent Society for Retarded Children-Willow-
brook Chapter, an affiliate of NYSARC, became a more militant group
and, according to one report, "has achieved the nominal right to have
a voice in all important policy decisions concerning the institutions."[38]
For its part, also as a defensive reaction to the Willowbrook stories,
the New York State Department of Mental Hygiene, "made unprecedented
overtures to parents, including establishing a Task Force to write
guidelines for patient and parents'rights for all state institutions for
the mentally retarded and mentally ill."[39] The Task Force, once
established, gradually assumed more power and forced the State
Commissioner to attend an emergency meeting where he was criticized
for an inadequate response to its recommendations—especially one
which called for a reallocation of budgeted funds toward community-
based, residential, after-care and rehabilitative services to the
mentally disabled.[40] This episode, which is not yet closed, is
illustrative of the latent power of consumer groups, which when allied
with politicos* can force a shift in control over health facilities.

CONCLUSION

Both the state and local health facilities discussed here and the
VA hospitals discussed in the previous chapter are by definition in
the public sector; there, however, the resemblance ends. In contrast
to the virtually monolithic administrative structure of the Veterans
Administration, state and local facilities, being organs of multiple

_____

*Then-Representative (later Governor) Hugh Carey chided the
Republican administration for viewing consumer representation as
"window-dressing."

political jurisdictions, are highly variegated. Again, unlike the VA
situation where a specific target population exists, state and local
units serve a heterogeneous population: the indigent, self-paying
patients, patients of both sexes with mental disturbances and addictions
of varying types and severity, of all ages and economic status. The
fragmented nature of the target populations has inhibited the development of consumer organizations, or where such do exist, they too
function along particularistic lines. Further, the multileveled and
labyrinthian characteristics of the controlling bureaucracies present
grave barriers to the focusing of accountability questions. As in the
case of the VA hospitals, civil service procedures limit the kinds of
sanctions that can be imposed on middle- and lower-echelon function-
aries and on some upper-level ones as well.

It appears, then, that general administrative reorganization and
functional rethinking are the prerequisites for improvement in the
accountability mechanisms of state and local units. On these questions
more will be said subsequently.

NOTES

1. Appendix A, Table A-1, p. 143.

2. Appendix C, Table C-1, p. 149.

3. The 1973 AMA Guide to the Health Care Field (Chicago:
American Hospital Association, 1973), p. 13.

4. Howard D. Young and Alex Rosen, New York City's Municipal
Hospital System: Physicians' Perceptions (New York: Design and
Evaluation, Inc., no date), p. 13.

5. Community Health Services for New York City, Report and
Staff Studies of the Commission on the Delivery of Personal Health
Services (Piel Commission) (New York: Praeger Publishers, 1969),
pp. 17-18.

6. Ibid., p. 28.

7. Ibid., pp. 28-9. Also, "Many Foreign Physicians in U.S.
Found Unlicensed," New York Times, June 20, 1974.

8. New York Times, June 25, 1974, p. 20.

9. Eli Ginsberg et al Urban Health Services: The Case of New
York (New York: Columbia University Press, 1971), p. 97.

10. New York City's Municipal Hospital System . . .,op. cit.,
p. 21.

11. Ibid., p. 51.

12. See for example "The Politics of Mental Retardation,"
Health/PAC Bulletin, January 1973.

13. Civil Rights of Mental Patients Are Debated by Medical and
Legal Professors," New York Times, March 25, 1974. See also

Jones Robitscher, "Courts, State Hospitals and the Right to Treatment," American Journal of Psychiatry 129, no. 3 (September 1972).

14. Herbert E. Klarman, Hospital Care in New York City (New York: Columbia University Press, 1963), p. 316.

15. Summarized in Alice Tetelman, "Public Hospitals—Critical or Recovering," Health Services Reports 88, no. 4 (April 1973).

16. Ibid., p. 296.

17. Community Health Services for New York City, op. cit.

18. Robb K. Burlage, New York City's Municipal Hospitals: A Policy Review (Washington, D.C.: Institute for Policy Studies, 1967).

19. See note 4.

20. Alan F. Charles, "Improving the Quality of Care in Municipal Hospitals," in Materials on Health Law, vol. 2, The Hospital, prepared by the Health Law Project, University of Pennsylvania Law School, rev. ed., 1972, p. 412.

21. Milton I. Roemer and Jay W. Friedman, Doctors in Hospitals (Baltimore: Johns Hopkins Press, 1971), p. 27.

22. Charles M. Brecher and Miriam Astow, "Ambulatory Services," in Eli Ginsberg et al., Urban Health Services, op. cit., p. 139.

23. John W. Gardes, "Anticipated Directions for the Future of Public General Hospitals," American Journal of Public Health 59, no. 4 (April 1969), p. 684.

24. Tetelman, op. cit., pp. 296-297.

25. Ibid., p. 297.

26. Ibid., p. 298.

27. Klarman, op. cit., p. 388; Annual Report of the New York City Health and Hospitals Corporation, July 1, 1972—June 30, 1973, pp. 121-122.

28. "Highlights of 1972," New York State Department of Mental Hygiene (mimeo), p. 2.

29. Anne R. Somers, "State Regulation of Hospitals and Health Care: The New Jersey Story," Blue Cross Reports Research Series II, July 1973, passim.

30. "The Cost of Health Care in New York State," Six Month Interim Report prepared by The Temporary State Commission on Living Costs and the Economy, April 1974.

31. Ibid., pp. 42-43.

32. "Highlights of 1972," op. cit., p. 6.

33. "Annual Report of the New York City Health and Hospitals Corporation," op. cit.

34. Ibid.

35. "The Cost of Health Care . . .," op. cit., p. 3.

36. Annual Report of the New York City Health and Hospitals Corporation," op. cit., p. 12.

37. Tetelman, op. cit., p. 301.
38. "The Politics of Mental Retardation," op. cit., p. 16.
39. Ibid., p. 17.
40. New York Times, October 29, 1974, p. 41.

In this chapter we move away from the public and from the not-for-profit sectors in the health field to the so-called for-profit or proprietary sector. * The difference between the two sectors is implied in the titles: for-profit facilities are owned and operated with the stated intention of producing a net profit which inures to the owner, whether the latter be a single entrepreneur, partnership, or corporation. (When not-for-profit facilities have an excess of revenue over cost, the excess may not be appropriated by any individual or group.) Operating a facility for profit implies further that the profit sought should be a maximum and that it should compare favorably with the return on any alternative opportunity for the investment of funds. In other words, the health facility is a business, like any other; it is subject to the same rules and regulations applicable to any business firm and its revenues and properties are taxable by all levels of government.

No sooner do we set out the definition however, than qualifications emerge. One writer noted for example that most proprietary hospitals, "were established by physicians as a community service, rather than investment."[1] Although it is difficult to disentangle all of the motives

---

*The authors of an American Hospital Association monograph, "Study of For-Profit Hospital Chains" (1970) eschew the proprietary term since, legalisticaly, even not-for-profit facilities are owned by some one or some group. In the present work the terms are used interchangably, as they are in common usage.

for setting up the early private hospitals, we are inclined, for the sake of argument, to accept the above statement but to point out that what may have been true historically, when hospitals were scarce or nonexistent, does not hold for the present. The entry of large corporate entities into the hospital and nursing-home fields is dictated solely by the search for profits—although in some few cases, physicians in isolated areas may still be motivated in part by community service and by concern for their own convenience in establishing hospitals or other health facilities.

We do not propose in the present chapter to discuss the normative questions involved in the profit/not-for-profit controversy in the health field. Our task here as throughout is to focus on proprietary health facilities through the accountability prism. Using the format set out in the preceding chapters we shall discuss the two most important types of for-profit facilities—hospitals and long-term care facilities (nursing homes). The former case, incidentally, is one where the hospitals constitute a small minority of the total hospital universe, and the latter is one where proprietary facilities predominate.

PROPRIETARY HOSPITALS

General Description

The data in Appendix Tables A-1, A-2, and in C-1 enable us to sketch a functional profile of proprietary hospitals. The main characteristics that emerge are the following:

(a) The most usual type of care given in our hospitals is provided in short-term general facilities. As noted earlier, this area is largely preempted by the not-for-profit facilities. Proprietary hospitals rank third in this type of care, behind the nongovernmental-not-for-profit and local government facilities. This point deserves emphasis: in the short-term acute care field, proprietaries are not very significant in relative terms.[2]

(b) The area in which proprietary hospitals constitute the single most important factor is that of providing short-term psychiatric care. Here proprietaries rank first, with 47 percent of all hospitals compared with 33 percent for the nongovernmental, not-for-profit types. This differential does not persist, however, in the beds, admissions, and outpatient categories, suggesting that the proprietary facilities though more numerous are generally smaller in size.

(c) Interestingly, the dominance in the short-term psychiatric field is not carried over into the long-term psychiatric area. In this field, the for-profits maintain an equal rank with voluntaries (11 percent) but both are far behind the 60 percent represented by state government units. (See Chapter 3.)

(d) Proprietaries as well represented in short-term specialty hospitals, ranking second behind voluntaries—27 and 62 percent respectively.

(e) There is only one area where proprietaries do not exist at all, and that is the long-term tuberculosis and other respiratory disease facilities.

Viewed over the 1946 to 1972 time span, proprietaries showed a 31 percent decrease in the number of hospitals, but increases were recorded in beds, admissions, and outpatient visits. In relative terms, proprietaries decreased from 18 percent of all hospitals in 1946 to 10 percent in 1972; increased slightly in terms of beds—from 3 to 4 percent; decreased in admissions from 9 to 7 and increased slightly in outpatient visits—3 to 4 percent. [3] Clearly, with 10 percent of all hospitals and 4 percent of the beds we are dealing with a relatively small segment of the hospital field. On a less aggregate level, however, there is evidence that proprietary hospitals are more prevalent in urban than in rural areas. In New York City, for example, proprietary facilities constitute more than 25 percent of all hospitals. [4]

Internal Accountability

Legal

A 1970 report by the American Hospital Association noted that proprietary hospitals existed in all but eight states. [5] The most recent edition of Hospital Statistics (1972) reveals that North Dakota, one of the previous eight, now has one proprietary, leaving seven states in the "no proprietary" category. [6] Thus, while there is a pervasive bias among health planners and government officials against the existence of for-profit health care facilities, it appears that there are generally no widespread obstacles in the United States to their establishment and continued existence.

Under the general incorporation laws of the states therefore, a single entrepreneur partnership or corporation* may apply for a

---

*New York State is an exception. Under a 1967 Amendment to the Social Welfare Law "Any natural persons . . . " were permitted to establish and operate hospitals for profit, thus prohibiting stock

charter under procedures similar to those for any other business enterprise. There are some qualifications, however. All states would require the permission of either the State Health Department or the State Social Services Department to establish a health facility. In addition, some states require the consent of a state health planning agency and some have enacted "certificate-of-need" legislation which places the burden on the institutions to show that a need for the facility exists in a given community. Furthermore, 17 states prohibit so called chain-operated* health facilities from operating in their juris-dictions. Finally, some states which permitted proprietary corpora-tions did so by issuing waivers which specified that the facility was a limited service hospital. [7]

All of the legal constraints that were outlined in Chapter 1 above in connection with the voluntary hospital apply to the proprietaries as well. The exemptions from taxation which voluntaries enjoy, do not of course apply to proprietaries, which like any other commercial enterprises are subject (as noted earlier) to real estate and income taxation by all levels of government.

Governance

In the case of governance, too, our treatment of proprietaries is similar in most respects to that accorded voluntaries. That is to say, each hospital has an administrator, chiefs of services (with numbers depending on size and variety of services offered), heads of nursing services, and the like. However, the important difference in governance between the voluntaries and proprietaries is the ex-istence of an "owner" who has ultimate control and responsibility over the facility. In some cases the owner will operate in conjunction with a board of directors; in other cases, usually in the smaller hospital, there will not be a board. If the owner is a closed corporation

---

corporations (public or not) from operating in the field (see Note 5). The anomaly now exists that M. D. s and D. D. S. s are permitted to form professional corporations (P. C.), in effect permitting single person corporations to render care on a one-to-one basis, but denying that right (privilege?) to multiperson corporations.

*"Chain-operated" refers to multifacility ownership of hospitals often across state lines, by a single, controlling (usually publicly held) corporation.

composed of more than one individual, then control will rest with an
executive committee; if not with the corporation's president. In the
case of a corporation which has issued stock to the public, the stockholders theoretically are the owners of the corporation; but as is the
case with corporations generally, control resides in the president,
or occasionally in a strong board of directors. Day-to-day operations
are the responsibility of a second tier of managers (Gailbraith's
technostructure) who exercise a great deal of de facto control. Most
boards of directors of large, corporate owned health facilities, will
include at least one or more M. D. s.

It may be appropriate at this juncture to raise a point which has
both governance and ethical aspects. This is the question of ownership of the hospital by a physician (mentioned above) who may be the
sole owner, or the ownership by a group of physicians in a given
community. The obvious problem in these cases is a potential conflict of interest. [8] Will not a physician who owns stock in a hospital
send patients there who (a) belong in other, more appropriate facilities
or (b) who should not be in a hospital at all? Further, since the
physician has a proprietary interest, will he not tend to overlook or
cover up abuses or instances of malfeasance or malpractice? A full
discussion of these issues is of course beyond the scope of our present
study. Protection of the public against abuses in such a situation derives from two sources: one is the physicians' own system of ethics
and morality, the other is full disclosure of the proprietary interests
to patients, to health officials, and to the public generally.

One final point should be made here on legal governance accountability questions. Where ownership of proprietary facilities by publicly
held corporations is involved, a full registration statement pertaining
to the sales of the shares must be made with the Securities and Exchange Commission (intrastate offerings involving less than $300,000
are registered with the State Securities Department only). Relevant
material from the registration statement is presented in a prospectus
which all potential buyers of an initial stock offering should receive
and hopefully, study. The SEC statement is concerned primarily with
financial disclosure, and in some cases it will also alert stockholders
and the public to potential conflict of interest among principals, board
members, and the corporate entity. Experience indicates however,
that prospectuses are rarely given intensive scrutiny, so that in the
important case of health care additional avenues of disclosure may be
needed.

Stockholders also receive annual reports containing balance sheets
and income statements, and though perhaps less forbidding than
prospectuses, these receive little more knowledgable scrutiny.

Professional Accountability

Perhaps the best approach to an evaluation of professional account-ability is that developed by Roemer and Friedman in their typology of Medical Staff Organization (1950).* "It should be noted," these authors state, "that the sponsorship of the hospital (government, voluntary nonprofit, or proprietary) is not strictly relevant to evalua-tion of the MSO. There is no theoretical reason why any form of sponsorship cannot be associated with any degree of MSO, even though we know that in practice government general hospitals are more likely to have highly structured staffs, voluntary hospitals moderately structured ones and proprietary hospitals the most loosely structured staffs. There are, nevertheless, some small proprietary hospitals with highly organized medical staffs.[9] Generalizations concerning proprietaries as a group should, consequently, be made with a great deal of caution.

It may be well to point out that in large metropolitan areas many physicians have dual affiliations, the primary affiliation being with a large voluntary hospital and secondary ones with proprietaries. Three major reasons for proprietary affiliation may be adduced: (1) the need for beds which may be in short supply in the voluntaries, (2) the fact that the patient's illness is not complex and can be treated just as well in these hospitals, and (3) proprietary stays are less expensive. The consequence of this affiliation pattern is that highly qualified physicians who insist on minimum quality standards will exert a positive effect on the proprietaries, and they may possibly also have an educational impact on less qualified physicians. Need-less to say, these conditions do not apply in rural or semirural areas where large voluntaries, medical schools, or teaching hospitals are not accessible.

Actually, if we use data on hospital approvals and affiliations as indicative of the level of professional activity, proprietary hospitals are found wanting. Referring to Table A-2 in Appendix A, we note

---

*The seven components comprising an MSO index are composition of staff, appointment procedure, commitment, departmentalization, control committees, documentation, and informal dynamics. (Roemer and Friedman, p. 87.)

that proprietary hospitals have the lowest percentage of JCAH accreditations and almost no other type of accreditation with the exception of eligibility for participation in Blue Cross and Medicare, yet, as Steinwald and Neuhauser have shown, "when size is controlled for, there is not too much difference in the percentage of proprietary and nonproprietary hospitals which are accredited.[10] (A counterargument here is the fact that there are very few proprietaries in the 300 plus bed size class.)[11] Moreover, as the same authors point out, "it is interesting to note that all the characteristics of proprietary hospitals measured here [such as total hospitals, total beds, mean bed size, average occupancy, average length of stay, average total expense per patient day, average assets per bed for the period 1960-68] with the exception of total expense per patient day, have been moving closer to the means of these measures for voluntary hospitals. This is suggestive that hospitals are becoming more homogeneous, but it is certainly not conclusive."[12]

Additional supportive evidence of the homogeneity tendency is provided by the application of a so-called death-rate-adjusted-for-case mix index of quality of care to a sample of voluntaries and proprietaries in California. This test did not show any clear case of voluntary superiority.[13] (The reader may be reminded here of the tendency toward convergence between governmental and nongovernmental hospitals noted in Chapter 3).

For some purposes it is useful to distinguish between "chain-operated" and other proprietary hospitals. While the former (as of a 1969 study) were only 21 percent of all for-profit hospitals, they appear to be growing in absolute and relative importance.[14] Without entering into a discussion of the pros and cons of multiple facility corporate ownership, we simply present here Ferber's main findings from an AHA study of such chains:[15]

> The hospitals acquired and operated by the chains
> differ from the other for-profit hospitals: they tend
> to be larger, they include a somewhat greater pro-
> portion of AHA members, and they are more often
> located in metropolitan areas. The chain hospitals,
> especially in the smaller size categories, compare
> well with or exceed the other for-profit hospitals in
> accreditation and medical certification. They had
> higher personnel ratios and higher figures for ex-
> penses per in-patient day and expense per admission
> than the other for-profit hospitals, and except in the
> largest hospitals, higher payroll expense per employee.

On the basis of these features, a tentative conclusion is that the chain-operated proprietaries show even greater homogeneity with respect to voluntaries than do nonchain proprietaries.

Flow of Funds

This discussion of fund flow is, of necessity, conjectural, since we have not seen any studies in this area. Our presumption is that since proprietaries seek, among other things, to maximize profits, and since they are subject to taxation, their internal accounting and financial control procedures are more systematic and tighter than is true of their voluntary counterparts. Bernard Korman, president of American Medicorp, one of the largest of the hospital chains, put it this way: "The hospitals that are losing money do so because their management methods are largely historical in origin, including basic inefficiencies and no incentives to hold costs down."[16]

The necessity of preparing income tax returns annually as well as Annual Reports—and in some cases semiannual or quarterly reports—implies that certain standard and consistent accounting practices will be followed, if for no other reasons than compliance with Internal Revenue, SEC, and state and local requirements. Proprietaries therefore possess these additional layers of fiscal responsibility and accountability which are absent from voluntaries and often from governmental units as well.

External Accountability

Legal—Governance

Little need be added here to what has already been said regarding legal accountability. On the matter of governance however, it would be well to point out that the allegations we noted in Chapter 1 with respect to the unrepresentativeness and self-perpetuation of Board members applies a fortiori to proprietaries. Closely held for-profits need account to no one for board membership, where boards exist at all. Publicly held hospital corporations, on the other hand, are required to hold annual elections, but as in most such cases the slate presented by the incumbent management usually prevails. Even if large numbers of stockholders were to vote in an entirely new board of directors, it is questionable what groups the new directors would represent; most certainly it would not be the community-at-large.

Quality and Functional Accountability

In apparent disregard of their own caveats regarding a priori assumptions based on control types, Roemer and Friedman have the following to say concerning proprietaries:[17]

> Sponsorship of a hospital by private individuals for profit sets (other) probable limits on the range of functions. Proprietary hospitals have little motivation to serve the poor, to provide education, do research or maintain relationships with other community agencies. With profit as a motive, the objective becomes to maximize services that yield income and minimize those that do not. The wishes of the private doctor, whose good-will brings in the patients, have top priority; hence hospital activities that might be construed as "competing" with private practice (such as out-patient x-rays for private patients) are avoided.

The pejorative term "cream skimming" has been applied to the activities (or lack of them) described by Roemer and Friedman. Proprietaries tend to admit only self-pay or fully insured patients, eschew complex cases and do not as a rule have emergency rooms, outpatient clinics, pediatric and obstetric services, and they avoid cardiac cases as well. Following usual rational behavior, for-profits tend to eliminate or do not take on any services which customarily produce losses. Nevertheless, as we indicated earlier, quality differences between profits and not-for-profits within bed size ranges of (say) 100 to 200 beds are virtually nonexistent. The "cream skimming" charge is probably true but it may be well to recall that voluntaries have been accused of the same practice by local government hospitals—the so-called "dumping" allegation noted above. The lack of ethics in both cases becomes a matter of degree.

Critics of the health care system in the United States often raise the issue of duplication of facilities which abounds in the voluntary hospital sector. Yet when proprietary hospitals refuse to provide certain services which may already be provided by voluntaries in a given area they are subject to criticism. The question may well be raised why the elimination of duplication is not a rational action and why it will not lead to a more efficient allocation of resources in the health sector as a whole.

Chain-operated proprietaries carry rationalization even further. Interstate multifacility hospitals are coordinated by a central authority and are thus able to take advantage of large-scale purchasing, construction economies, and the possibility of obtaining capital in large

amounts at relatively low costs. Again, lack of coordination and of
shared services and facilities have been high on the agenda of health
critics. Should it be a cause of complaint when they are achieved?
Perhaps the issue may be seen more clearly if we assume a completely
planned health care system. Would we not take advantage of the well-
known principles of division of labor, of specialization, and of economies of scale? We are not taking any position here on profit versus
nonprofit activities but are raising a different, more fundamental
question of the optimum allocation of resources. Social intervention
is justifiable in the situation where proprietaries do not wish to provide certain basic health services such as emergency rooms in a
community which lacks them. Then we ought to apply a reverse
certificate-of-need criterion—no license to operate unless certain
services are provided. In any event, if proprietary operations per
se in the health field are called into question, the critiques, to be
seriously entertained, should be based on grounds other than economic
(and even health planning) rationality.

One area of valid criticism of proprietaries concerns the extent
to which they cooperate with comprehensive/health planning agencies—
so-called 314(b) agencies. An American Hospital Association survey
of this question undertaken in 1970 indicated that, "there is some
evidence that for-profit hospitals, particularly chain-operated for-
profit hospitals, do not participate in community planning to the
same extent as nonprofit hospitals."[18] Corrective action to remedy
this situation is certainly in order: legislation making it mandatory
to adhere to guidelines and regulations of state health planning agencies
in New York (see Appendix C-3) would seem to be the most appropriate
policy.

To the author's knowledge, there is no legislation that mandates
consumer participation in the affairs of proprietary health facilities,
and our assumption is therefore that consumer inputs are rare or
nonexistent. Consumer complaints to health departments and malpractice suits are, of course, as prevalent in proprietaries as elsewhere.

EXTENDED CARE FACILITIES

General Description

The Department of Health, Education, and Welfare defines nursing
homes as, "establishments with three beds or more which provide
nursing or personal care to the aged, infirm, or chronically ill."[19]
In short, we are dealing here with something less than hospital care

but something other than care in the home, and also with facilities
which are largely proprietary in nature.

We stated earlier that in sharp contrast to the proprietary hospital
situation, the nursing home field is one where proprietaries are
dominant. Table D-1 in Appendix D presents some of the salient
characteristics of nursing homes. * Whereas proprietary hospitals
account for about 10 percent of all hospitals and only 4 percent of
all beds in the United States, proprietary nursing homes constitute
77 percent of all homes and 67 percent of all beds. Proprietaries are
particularly involved in personal care homes without nursing (86 percent) and in domiciliary care (80 percent). There are two areas in
which proprietaries are not the most important type, namely in (a)
the proportion of beds in personal care homes with nursing, where
nonprofits comprise 49 percent and proprietaries rank next with
38 percent, and (b) beds in domiciliary care homes where nonprofits
again rank first with 52 percent and proprietaries second with 43 percent. In 1971, according to the most recent data from the Master
Facility Inventory of HEW, the United States had 22,004 nursing homes
which "contained more than 1,200,000 beds and had 1,075,000 residents
(an occupancy rate of 90 percent)."[20] (There are, it is interesting
to note, almost as many nursing home beds as hospital beds—1,507,588
in the latter with an average occupancy rate of 79 percent).[21]

Internal Accountability

Legal and Governance

Historically (in New York State and probably elsewhere) proprietary
nursing homes developed out of private family homes which were used
for sick, homeless, or aged people. As a result of existing and potential demand, these homes grew rapidly. "Yet," as one author pointed
out, "they were not part of any health care system and were virtually
unregulated."[22]

In New York State, parenthetically, proprietary nursing homes
may not be incorporated, since (as mentioned earlier in the present
chapter) the "corporate practice of medicine" is prohibited. (By a

----

*This table was based on preliminary data. The data in the final
report (see note 19) show some differences, but they are not
appreciable.

curious inversion of terminology, incorporated nursing homes are nonprofit institutions.) This situation, however, is in all probability unique to New York.

In New York it was not until 1951 that " . . . legislation providing for registration and inspection of these institutions was passed and a mild code of regulations promulgated."[23] The agency designated to administer the law, which required registration and not licensure, was the Board of Social Welfare. Finally by the Metcalf-McCloskey and Folsom Acts of 1964 and 1965 all health institutions in New York State were required to have the approval of the State Public Health Council and to be subject to the authority of the New York State Department of Health.

As private enterprises, proprietary nursing homes—with the exception of those owned and operated by publicly held corporate entities—are not required to adhere to any prescribed governance patterns. However, those homes which seek accreditation from the Joint Commission for the Accreditation of Hospitals and those which seek certification for participation in the Medicare and Medicaid programs must meet certain standards pertaining to governance and administration of the facilities. These matters, being responses to external pressures, are described below.

Professional Accountability

Dr. Martin Cherkasky, in the Foreword to William Thomas' study, stated that "the real disaster in nursing home care has been its isolation from the hospital."[24] The consequence of this isolation has been brought to the attention of the public rather forcefully in descriptions of the inadequate (bordering on the criminal) medical care and supervision in nursing homes that have appeared in the Congressional Record, in Congressional Hearings, in newspaper stories, in Nader Reports, and in recently published books.[25]

To cite one case, Claire Townsend reported on the epidemic of Salmonella in one nursing home which resulted in the death of 25 and the illness of another 108 patients. The epidemic was reported 4 days after it became manifest largely because there was no continuous communication between M.D.s who had patients in the home and the house staff. An investigative panel set up by the Maryland Secretary of Health and Mental Hygiene concluded that there was no overall medical supervision, that doctors saw only their own patients and did not consult with the nursing home staff. No single M.D. was held responsible for the outbreak or for not reporting the incident.[26] The home (Gould Convalesarium) had a titular, "principal physician" who, perhaps in theory, was responsible for overall medical supervision but who in practice turned out to be a physician who treated patients not having their own doctors.

Cases of the kind just described are bound to occur where there are no full-time or even part-time physicians on the premises of the nursing home, or where they are not available on very short notice. Congressman David Pryor stated the case in stark terms: "The doctor an anonymous shadow and unseen visitor, is actually only a mirage in a desert of despair. The atmosphere is a culture of death, not life."[27]

The person, however, who is most closely associated with the home is the Administrator. "He is the one who carries out the policies of the directors of the establishment and sets the tone for the type and quality of service that residents in the institution receive."[28]

Of particular interest here are some of the characteristics of nursing home administrators found in the 1968 study just cited.

- Proprietary institutions had the highest proportion of administrators with a high school education or less and the lowest proportion of administrators with a college or graduate education.
- Proprietary institutions averaged the largest proportion of administrations without a degree, license or certificate.
- Proprietary institutions had the lowest proportion of administrators with five years or more of previous administrative experience.

Given these characteristics of both professional medical supervisors and of the qualifications of administrators, one would have to conclude that there were only minimal degrees of internal responsibility and accountability in proprietary nursing homes. As a coordinator of medical services in Denver, Colorado, put it: "Except for requirements on records, quality of medical care is not regulated. No county welfare department or medical society maintains medical review teams. The medical discipline in hospitals and other institutions with organized medical staffs is conspicuous by its absence in nursing homes."[29] The situation changed and is changing under the impact of external legislation, namely the 1967 amendments to Title XIX (effective 1970) requiring the licensing of administrators, but more on this below.

Fiscal Accountability

Just as there was laxity in medical supervison and in administration of proprietary nursing homes, so was there a great deal of fiscal irresponsibility. The literature mentioned in note 25 abounds with incidents of financial chicanery. Most of the abuses documented occurred in the pre-Medicare-Medicaid era but undoubtedly not a few of them still persist.

A portion of an article that appeared in the Detroit <u>News</u> and which was entered into the <u>Congressional Record</u> by Representative Martha W. Griffiths is illustrative:[30]

> The owner of that place would steal from the patients. There was this one man—he came to the home in a taxi-cab from Harper Hospital. And to my amazement he had $190 in cash in his pocket, which was most unusual. The head nurse and I counted the money and we put it in a valuables envelope and put it away for safekeeping. So in comes the owner, and he doesn't say "Hello" or "How are you?" or "Where's the new patient?" or anything. The first thing he says is: "How much money did he have and where is it?"
>
> The next morning I came in and the money was gone. Two weeks later, the guy dies. Know who paid for the funeral? The state! Know where the $190 went? Into the bank—the owner's personal account. I know. I did all the banking.

In her 1974 muckracking expose of the nursing home industry, <u>Tender Loving Greed,</u> Mary Adelaide Mendelson reported a great deal of concealed ownership in the industry. "Finding out who owns nursing homes—who makes the decisions and who rakes in the profits—is an extremely difficult undertaking."[31]

External Accountability

Legal and Governance

Enactment of the Medicare and Medicaid Acts (Titles 18 and 19 of the Social Security Act), with their huge infusion of new funds, has served as an important agent of change in the entire health care system, nursing homes included. While "the law never intended to pay for ordinary nursing home care," as the Somers [32] have noted, the pro-portion of such homes is quite low. An overwhelming proportion of existing homes qualified immediately to receive government funds either as extended or intermediate care facilities and others began to upgrade quickly in order to meet the eligibility requirements for participation in the programs. The JCAH in conjunction with the American Association of Homes for the Aging (representing nonprofits and governmentals) and the American Nursing Home Association (rep-resenting proprietaries chiefly) began in 1966 to set up accreditation procedures for nursing homes as they had done earlier for hospitals. [33]

The primary requirements for participation in the new federal programs were set out by the Social Security Administration. [34]

Of specific importance here are the SSA standards regarding legal and governance functions. The requirements for participation are that (a) "There is a governing body which assumes full legal responsibility for the overall conduct of the facility," and further that "the ownership of the facility is fully disclosed to the State agency." (In the case of corporations the corporate officers are made known.) Also, "the governing body is responsible for compliance with the applicable laws and regulations of legally authorized agencies." The requirements specify further that a full-time administrator be appointed and they set out the desirable (though not mandated) characteristics of such administrators. [35] In addition, Section 1908 (a) of Public Law 90-248 "requires that all states participating in the Medicaid program who wish to continue to receive federal funds must have a program for the licensing of administrators of long-term care institutions in effect by July 1, 1970."[36]

The above requirements undoubtedly resulted in tightening of the legal and governance situation in nursing homes, although, again, there are reports from numerous sources of lack of compliance with the regulations. By 1971 there were relatively few homes which did not meet the standards of administrative management outlines above. [37]

Quality and Functional Accountability

The main external force acting on quality of nursing homes is again the desire and necessity of obtaining government funds via Titles 18 and 19. In order to participate in these programs, extended care facilities must have, inter alia, (a) a transfer agreement with one or more hospitals, (b) a group of professional personnel guiding the policies of the facility, (c) a physician, a registered nurse, or a medical staff responsible for execution of policies, (d) a requirement that the health care of every patient must be under the supervision of a physician, (e) clinical records on all patients, (f) 24-hour nursing service, (g) appropriate procedures for dispensing drugs, and (h) a utilization review plan. [38] Another class of nursing homes termed "intermediate care facilities" were also eligible to participate, with less stringent conditions placed on them. Many more homes had deficiencies in these areas than in the areas mentioned. [39]

Apart from the legislative pressures to upgrade nursing home care, there are a number of organizations which carry on continuous educational programs in the field. Besides the Joint Commission and its association with the American Association of Homes for the Aging (AAHA) and the American Nursing Home Association (ANHA),

we might mention too the American College of Nursing Home Administrators and the Association of University Programs in Health Administration.[40]

An attempt by the author to determine the place that proprietary
homes had in general evaluations of nursing home quality proved un-
fruitful. The Joint Commission informed me that as of December 31,
1973, there were 1,726 long-term care facilities with JCAH accreditation but no information was provided on the proportion of these that
were proprietary.[41]

A statement entered into the Congressional Record by Representative Pryor included the following remarks on proprietary homes.[42]

> The expensive nursing homes are the best homes—
> clean, with shining medical equipment and thick carpet-
> ing, institutions such as those run by some 70 chain
> corporations that sell stocks on the public market . . .
> Even here—amidst the luxury of carpeting, the elder-
> ly will be handled by personnel who do not understand
> them, who will treat them as confused babies and not
> human beings. Here too Government patients are
> likely to get care that is poorer than that of private
> patients and charges may well be inflated simply be-
> cause the Government is footing the bill.

Despite the many exposes of the poor quality of care in nursing
homes, little of a remedial nature has been undertaken. Susan Jacoby
wrote that "according to a report being prepared by Senator Moss's
subcommittee on long-term care, only 579 out of more than 23,000
homes have lost their certification for Federal funds. . . . The
figures contrast sharply with the 1971 G.A.O. audit's finding of
serious violations in more than half of the inspected homes."[43]

The bulk of federal monies flowing into nursing homes is derived
from the Medicaid program, and since this program involves cost-
sharing between the federal government and the states, threats to
cut off or reduce the federal share have potential leverage in the
system. Under new statutory changes to Title XIX, the federal government threatens to reduce its share of Medicaid payments to the states
unless the "State title XIX agency makes a showing satisfactory to the
Secretary that it has in operation an effective program of control over
utilization of such services. A satisfactory showing must include
evidence that[44]

1. A physician certifies as to each patients need for inpatient
   services at time of admission, or, if later, the time the patient
   applies for medical assistance, and recertifies as to such need
   at least every 60 days.

2. For each patient, the services are furnished under a plan
   established and periodically reviewed and evaluated by a
   physician.
3. The state has in effect a continuous utilization review (UR)
   program whereby each patient's admission to and continued
   stay in the institution are reviewed and evaluated (with such
   frequency as may be prescribed in Federal regulations) by
   medical and other professional personnel not themselves
   directly responsible for the patient's care.
4. The State has an effective program of medical review (MR)
   in mental hospitals and SNFs, and independent professional
   review (IPR) in ICFs, providing a review of each patient's
   care at least annually.

The Secretary must validate the state's showing by conducting
sample onsite surveys in the institutions.

(In the above quotation, SNF stands for Skilled Nursing Facilities and
ICF for Intermediate Care Facilities.)
    We may observe here a typical scenario. First, legislation which
generated considerable money flows (more than 3.5 billion annually),
then reported abuses, and finally attempts to remedy systemic faults
through the powerful leverage of withholding funds. The extent to
which such government attempts to monitor its funds as well as to
upgrade care will succeed depends on the scope and adequacy of the
surveillance effort as well as on the supply of nursing-home beds.
Under conditions of tight supply, with a few alternatives, even the
most ambitious program to remedy abuses will lose its force. And,
it should be added, efforts to upgrade care—including the physical
environment (safety, etc.) and personnel—will, unless offset by
efficiency increases, result in higher costs. [45]

Fiscal and Cost Accountability

    Some of the more egregious fiscal abuses in the nursing home
industry—abuses that are primarily, but not solely practiced in
proprietaries—are presented in the following excerpt from the 1969
Hearing of the Senate Finance Committee, quoted in Mary Adelaide
Mendelson's recent book: [46]

> Unnecessary services are being provided on a wide-
> spread basis in nursing homes. . . . The majority
> of the extended care facilities [nursing homes licensed
> for Medicare] participating in the program do not fully
> meet the standards set in the law and regulations.
> Evidence exists that "kickback" arrangements between

suppliers—such as pharmacies and physical thera-
pists—and nursing homes may be widespread. . . .
There is substantial evidence that many physicians
are engaging in the practice known as "gang visits"
to nursing home and hospital patients. Under this
practice a physician may see as many as 30, 40
and 50 patients in a day in the same facility—regardless of whether the visit is medically necessary or
whether any service is actually furnished. . . .
Another cause for concern is the alarming growth
of chain operations in the nursing home field. Some
of these chains actively solicit physician purchase
of stock to assure a high occupancy rate. Other
chains purchase stock of hospital supply and pharma-
ceutical supply houses. This leads to arrangements
with respect to intercompany sales at what may very
well be higher than would otherwise be paid— a form
of captive market used to milk the Medicare trust
funds. . . . We have found inflated depreciation
allowances and many sales of facilities at inflated
prices in order to get maximum payments from
Medicare.

Each of the abuses mentioned in the above quotation virtually
suggests its own corrective. Foremost, perhaps is the need to eliminate any vestige of a cost-plus reimbursement system. Second,
more use must be made of the certificate-of-need concept, not only
with respect to the establishment and continuation of the facilities
themselves, but also for physician visits (a utilization review system
may be seen as a component of a general certificate-of-need process).
Finally, a complete disclosure of all financial transactions in the
facilities must be demanded. Enforcement of these measures, of
course, requires a vast increase in internal surveillance and external
inspection personnel, a better use of computerized systems to aid
in financial control and willingness to prosecute offenders and to de-
certify and ultimately to close homes that persist in perpetuating
abuses. [47]

Interfacility Accountability

As noted earlier, Medicare participation requires that extended
care facilities have a transfer agreement with a hospital. The benefits
of affiliation between the two types of institutions are obvious. One
author cited the following advantages:[48]

Aside from consideration of cost savings to the
community and to individual patients, availability
of specialized patient care directed towards rehabilitative needs, and reduction of length of stay
in general hospital beds, the affiliation of a
general hospital with an ECF provides the community with an effective combination of institutions
allowing a continuity of treatment for the patient
from the time of hospitalization until he regains
his health. The physical proximity of such affiliated
institutions, together with an effective formal relationship, has the effect of spreading the talents
and skills of specialized professional and para-
medical personnel to larger numbers of patients
and prevents costly duplication of facilities.

Herman and Anne Somers see additional positive features of the
Medicare induced interfacility cooperation, namely, that the extended
care facility may " . . . develop into a permanent satellite arrangement" and that the hospital " . . . may be encouraged to develop its
own EFC. "[49]

Consumer Accountability

Given that there are approximately three times as many nursing
homes as hospitals, that they are relatively small and widely scattered,
that they cater to a specialized kind of patient, and that resident turnover is low, nursing homes have not become the target of consumer
groups to the degree that hospitals have. However, demographic
imperatives and Titles 18 and 19 are gradually bringing nursing homes
into the same arena of public discussion and concern. Since 1972,
for example, HEW regulations require that inspectors' reports of
nursing homes be made public. (Due to the dual nature of the programs,
Medicare reports on individual homes are available at local Social
Security offices, while reports prepared for Medicaid purposes may
be seen at local welfare offices.) In reality, there is such a lack of
inspection personnel that in one internal memorandum a New York
State official complained, " . . . some upstate hospitals had not been
inspected in twenty years. "[50]
    A proposal to the Social Security Administration by New York
State Health officials that would mandate the posting of inspection
reports on the premises of each home was unfortunately rejected. [51]
In Rhode Island, a 1973 bill that was passed over the objections of
the nursing home lobby required "unannounced nursing home inspections, fines of up to $300 for each violation and total public access

to the inspection reports."[52] At a minimum, this kind of law should
be enacted by all of the states, and since as one legislator pointed
out, there are many more senior citizens than nursing home owners,
the necessary political clout is potentially available.

In order to augment the numbers of investigative personnel, an
imaginative, federally initiated, "Ombudsman Project" will train
older citizens as nursing home inspectors; the project is to be admin-
istered by the National Council of Senior Citizens.[53]

Finally, many organizations have prepared so-called "shopping
guides" to nursing homes including one by the Department of Health,
Education, and Welfare.[54]

The nursing home situation, for all of the reasons mentioned,
needs a more urgent consumer pressure group in order to achieve
reforms. One cannot help but agree with Edward P. Beard, a Rhode
Island legislator, who observed:

> . . . It's going to take real consumer pressure from
> the ground up to make them publicize the real dope.
> Flood each nursing home with people in their 60's
> demanding a look at the facilities. Have them camp
> out on the owners' doorsteps. It'll work.[55]

CONCLUSION

Seeking profits by setting up facilities to provide hospital or
nursing home care raises a number of important issues in the area
of accountability. One the one hand, the hospital or home must yield
an acceptable return on investment to remain viable—that is, the
owners cannot turn to philanthropists or to community fund drives to
remedy deficits. On the other, health care is so sensitive an area
that society does not permit market forces alone to shape decisions
concerning the nature of the services rendered. In the case of proprietary hospitals, we have seen that they are not significant from
a quantitative point of view and that they appear to be approaching the
level of care rendered in the average hospital of comparable size.

Since comprehensive health planning agencies are not functioning
at optimal levels in most states, proprietary hospitals, in all probability, are subject to less regulation than their voluntary counterparts. Federal funds via Medicare and Medicaid and insurance
payment, however, are important and carry with them regulatory
constraints that are undoubtedly increasing. Consumer inputs are
either nonexistent or negligible, since presumably the consumer
exercises a choice with respect to the hospital. The selection of

cases to be treated and the range of treatment provided is such that no great public outcry may be anticipated from the results—based on criteria of quality or cost.

Proprietary nursing homes paint an entirely different picture— they are the dominant mode of care; their care is realtively expensive; they have not been subject to the same regulatory agencies or degrees of standard enforcement as have hospitals; their patients generally suffer from chronic conditions (physical or mental) associated with aging; and the quality of care, which may easily be observed by visitors, has been and is of a kind to evoke widespread indignation and protest. More so than hospitals, nursing homes of all types are dependent on federal funds via Title 18 and 19, so that quality upgrading can be achieved most directly by appropriate standard setting and enforcement.

Recent attempts to increase accountability in nursing homes through such devices as receivership and by the organization of patients are assessed in Chapter 6.

NOTES

1. David A. Stewart, "The History and Status of Proprietary Hospitals," Blue Cross Reports, Research Series No. 9, March 1973, p. 3.

2. Appendix C, C-1.

3. Appendix A, A-1.

4. Hospitals and Related Facilities in Southern New York, 1973, Health and Hospital Planning Council of Southern New York, Inc., p. 5.

5. James R. Neely et al., "Study of For-Profit Hospital Chains," American Hospital Association, 1970 (mimeo) p. 69.

6. Hospital Statistics 1972, American Hospital Association, Table 5.

7. John T. Foster, "Proprietary Hospitals Go Public," Modern Hospital, March 1969, p. 86.

8. See "What's Good for the Common Stock is Good for the Common Duct," Modern Hospital, March 1969, editorial.

9. Milton I. Roemer and Jay W. Freedman, Doctors in Hospitals (Baltimore: Johns Hopkins Press, 1971), pp. 91-92.

10. Bruce Steinwald and Duncan Neuhauser, "The Role of the Proprietary Hospital," Law and Contemporary Problems 35, no. 10 (Autumn 1970), p. 821.

11. Hospital Statistics 1972, op. cit., Table 3.

12. Steinwald and Neuhauser, op. cit., p. 823.

13. David A. Stewart, op. cit., p. 6. See also Daniel B. Hill and David A. Stewart, "Proprietary Hospital versus Nonprofit

Hospitals: A Matched sample Analysis in California," Blue Cross Reports, March, 1973.

14. Bernard Ferber, "An Analysis of Chain-operated For Profit Hospitals," Health Services Research 6, no. 1, pp. 49 ff. See also Hirsch S. Ruchlin, Dennis D. Pointer, and Lloyd L. Cannedy, "A Comparison of For-Profit Investor-Owned Chain and Nonprofit Hospitals," Inquiry 10, no. 2 (December 1973), pp. 13-23.

15. Ibid., p. 59.

16. David M. Cleary, "American Medicorp: How to Make Money in the Hospital Business," Modern Hospital, March 1969, p. 92.

17. Roemer and Freedman, op. cit., p. 26.

18. Neely et al., op. cit., pp. 72-73.

19. "Inpatient Health Facilities as Reported from the 1971 MFI Survey," Department of Health, Education, and Welfare, Publication No. HRA 74-1807, March 1974, p. 1.

20. Ibid., p. 2.

21. Ibid., p. 33.

22. William C. Thomas, Jr., Nursing Homes and Public Policy: Drift and Decision in New York State (Ithaca, N.Y.: Cornell University Press, 1969), p. 6.

23. Ibid., p. 7.

24. Ibid., p. ix.

25. Some illustrations are: Ralph Nader et al., Nursing Homes for the Aged: The Agony of One Million Americans," Task Force Report on Nursing Homes, Center for Study of Responsive Law, Washington, D.C., 1970; Claire Townsend, Old Age: The Last Segregation (1971); Mary Adelaide Mendelson, Tender Loving Greed, 1974; Susan Jacoby, "Waiting for the End: On Nursing Homes," New York Times Magazine, March 31, 1974; Trends in Long Term Care, hearings before the Subcommittee on Long Term Care of the Special Committee on Aging, United States Senate, Ninety First Congress, Washington, 1970; and the four-part series in the New York Times beginning October, 1974.

26. Townsend, op. cit., p. 76.

27. Representative David H. Pryor in the Congressional Record, August 3, 1970, p. 27037.

28. "Characteristics of Administrators of Long-Term Care Institutions," Long Term Care Monograph No. 3 (Washington, D.C.: George Washington University, December 1969), p. 1.

29. Peter Samac, cited in Nursing Homes 14 (October 1965), p. 38.

30. Remarks of the Honorable Martha W. Griffiths, Congressional Record, March 16, 1970, p. 7530.

31. Mendelson, op. cit., p. 103.

32. Herman M. Somers and Anne R. Somers, Medicare and the Hospitals (Washington, D.C.: Brookings Institution, 1967), p. 67.

33. "Standards for Accreditation of Extended Care Facilities, Nursing Care Facilities," Joint Commission on Accreditation of Hospitals, Chicago, January 1968, p. iii.

34. Social Security Administration, Regulations No. 5, Subpart K, "Conditions of Participation; Extended Care Facilities."

35. Ibid., Sect. 405.1121, p. 11-67.

36. Pryor, op. cit., pp. 21-22.

37. Trends in Long Term Care, op. cit., pp. 2058-2059.

38. "Standards for Accreditation . . .," op. cit., Sect. 405.1101.

39. Pryor, op. cit., p. 2059ff.

40. See especially the AUPHA task force report, "Long Term Care: Opportunity and Challenge," by Theodore Litman, 1971; also "Education for Administration in Long Term Care Facilities," Proceedings of the First National Symposium on Long Term Care Administrator Education, April 1973.

41. Letter to the author from JCAH dated July 3, 1974.

42. Pryor, op. cit.

43. Susan Jacoby, "Waiting for the End . . . ," op. cit., p. 86.

44. Information Memorandum, Department of Health, Education, an and Welfare, Social and Rehabilitation Service, Washington, D.C., June 8, 1973.

45. Wallstreet Journal, January 14, 1974, p. 8.

46. Cited in Mendelson, op. cit., pp. 25-26.

47. For a discussion of some of the problems of surveillance and evaluation under Medicaid generally, see the collection of papers titled "Medicaid in New York: Utopianism and Bare Knuckles in Public Health," reprinted from American Journal of Public Health 59, no. 5 (May 1969).

48. Beaufort B. Longest, Jr., "Affiliation Agreements," Nursing Homes, November 1970, p. 16. See also "Guiding Principles for Agreements Between General Hospitals and Long-Term Care Facilities," American Hospital Association, 1964.

49. Somers and Somers, op. cit., p. 211.

50. Thomas, op. cit., p. 152.

51. Jacoby, op. cit., pp. 92-93.

52. Ibid., p. 92.

53. Mendelson, op. cit., p. 236.

54. "Nursing Home Care," Consumer Information Series No. 2, Department of Health, Education, and Welfare, Washington, D.C.

55. Jacoby, op. cit., p. 93.

5

NEIGHBORHOOD
HEALTH CENTERS

The present chapter differs from the previous chapters in that its focus is outpatient or ambulatory rather than inpatient care. While it is true that most hospitals offer some kind of outpatient facilities, "Ambulatory services," Brecher and Ostow commented, "received little professional attention and were almost a residual function of municipal and voluntary hospitals."[1] Perhaps the major factor inhibiting the growth of ambulatory services (as presently conceived) was the tradition of solo fee-for-service practice. Most persons when ill went to the local physician who, as a general practitioner, treated a wide range of diseases of all age groups and of both sexes. Several developments combined to render this traditional type of ambulatory care less viable. Among these may be mentioned the decline of the general practitioner concomitant with the growth of specialization; concentrations of poverty pockets in inner cities and the consequent movement of physicians to the suburbs; the increasing costs of medical care; the unwillingness (whether medically justifiable or not) of physicians to make house calls and the unavailability of physicians on holidays and on days off.

The response to these problems was the establishment, early in the twentieth century, of free-standing clinics and dispensaries which were usually sponsored by voluntary organizations—religious, charitable, and the like. Hospitals too expanded their outpatient departments, in part for humanitarian reasons but also for the education of interns and residents. The medical organizations both on a national scale and on local levels, opposed the spread of ambulatory services on the (usually unstated) ground of competition with local practitioners and on the notion of "free-choice" by the patient—a premise which rested on political-democratic as well as on economic-consumer sovereignty bases.

The demand for ambulatory services—as shown in Appendix A, Table A-1—grew more rapidly than population, number of hospitals, hospital beds, and admissions. With this increased demand, and in part because of it, criticisms of ambulatory services became more insistent. Hospital outpatient clinics were multispecialty in nature and not all the clinics operated simultaneously. This necessitated many trips to the hospital. Overcrowding led to long waits on the infamous wooden benches. The services were typically curative, not preventive. There was no outreach, and the care was fragmented and discontinuous.

While the defects of existing ambulatory care were being chronicled and criticized, another strand of research became prominent—the investigations into the mutually reinforcing linkage between poor health and poverty. It was natural therefore that when the "war on poverty" was officially declared by President Johnson in the 1960s the two strands would become interwoven. The attack on the health-poverty interlock took the form of the Neighborhood Health Center (NHC), which was sponsored and funded by the Office of Economic Opportunity as part of its Community Action Program.

These centers, * in the words of one government official, mark "the most extensive, concerted public effort in the history of the United States to expand ambulatory health care resources on a nationwide basis."[2] How these Neighborhood Health Centers show up when viewed through our accountability lens is the subject of the remainder of this chapter.

INTERNAL ACCOUNTABILITY

Legal and Governance

The multiplicity of goals envisioned by the Office of Economic Opportunity for neighborhood health centers may be gleaned from the following mandate:[3]

----

*At the time of this writing there were 118 Neighborhood Health Centers and 39 Family Health Centers. Personal communication to author from Health, Education, and Welfare Department dated May 29, 1974.

To be eligible for assistance, a comprehensive health
services project must:

1. . . . make possible, with maximum feasible use
of existing agencies and resources, the provision of
comprehensive health services, such as preventive,
diagnostic, treatment, rehabilitation, family planning,
narcotic addiction and alcoholism prevention and rehabilitation, mental health, dental and follow-up services;

2. . . . assure that these services are made readily
accessible to low-income residents of such areas, are
furnished in a manner most responsive to their needs
and with their participation, and whenever possible are
combined with, or included within, arrangements for
providing employment, education, social or other assistance needed by the families and individuals served.

In short, neighborhood health centers were to provide comprehensive services to the poor; to help mount an attack on poverty
through manpower training and the provision of employment, and to
accomplish these objectives with "maximum feasible participation"
of the target recipients.

Either existing public or voluntary agencies were eligible for
financial aid or de novo demonstration projects designed to fulfill
the OEO objectives could be established. Insofar as existing agencies
were involved, the legal and governance factors discussed in the
preceding chapter apply here as well. New projects were generally
organized as nonprofit community organizations. In states possessing
certificate-of-need legislation, approvals for new NHCs were routinely
given; first because of the demonstrated need for such services in
poor areas and second because federal funds would also be increased
to state (and local) health agencies which had been supporting health
services in the neighborhoods.

In terms of governance, OEO stipulated that "the governing board
of the administering agency is structured so that at least one-third
of its members are persons eligible to receive services from the
project," and that "a Neighborhood Health Council, which acts as a
policy advisory board to the administrative agency, is structured so
that at least one-half of its members are persons eligible to receive
services from the project;" and further that "the neighborhood residents
selected for the governing board and health council shall be democratically selected and their terms normally shall not exceed two
years."4

The Table of Organization of one of the oldest and most widely
studied of the NHCs, the Dr. Martin Luther King Jr. Health Center
(hereafter MLK), located in the borough of the Bronx in New York

City, pictured below, does not show an administration governing board but it does have a Community Advisory Board. The organization chart places the Community Advisory Board on a par with the Montefiore Hospital and Medical Center, with both bodies in a subordinate position to the Project and Deputy Project Directors. In fact however, the Montefiore Hospital is the grantee institution and OEO (now HEW) funds flow to it and from it to the Center itself. Far from a harmonious relationship, the Community Advisory Board has been in conflict with the OEO, the administration of the center itself, and the Local 1199 Hospital Workers Union over the issue of "community control."[5]

DR. MARTIN LUTHER KING, JR., HEALTH CENTER

TABLE OF ORGANIZATION

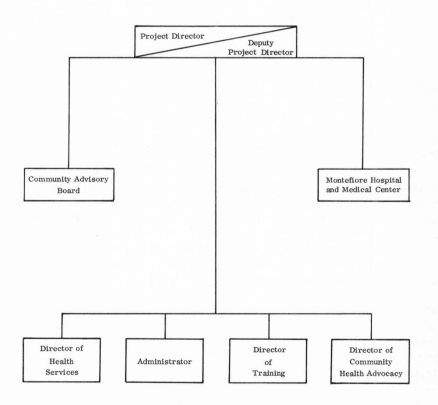

Source: Martin Luther King Jr. Health Center, Sixth Report, January 1972–July 1973, p. 1.

Similar conflicts over governance developed between the Health
Association (the community advisory board), the Health Center (the
administration) the OEO and the Tufts University Medical School, and
also between the OEO, the University of Southern California, and the
Community Health Council of the Social Central Multipurpose Health
Services Center in the Watts area of Los Angeles. [6] These illustrations
are not meant to decry community participation in health services;
rather they point up the need to delineate more clearly in advance
what the respective governance areas of the various components of
the NHCs are to be. Moreover, when population patterns shift, incumbent community representatives may be seen as no longer representing the community—a problem that plagues the MLK Center
with additional ethnic conflicts over control between black and Puerto
Rican groups. [7]

Professional Accountability

Neighborhood Health Centers present enormous problems of
professional accountability far more complex than those encountered
in any of our previously examined health facility institutions. There
problems arise from the complex multiple goals of the system, from
the innovative types of medical care practices (such as primary care
health team or home health care), from perceived and actual threats
to previously held notions of professional jurisdiction; from new administrative structures and from the forced interaction of professionals,
allied health personnel and indigent community workers. No surer
formula for internal conflict has ever been devised.

Harold Wise, a former project director of the MLK Center, put
it this way: "Given the immensity of the real problems faced by the
teams, given the fact that training of physicians and nurses is in
many ways inappropriate, even antithetical to the requirements of
team practice, given the diversity of cultural and economic back-
grounds of team members, we should have anticipated trouble."[8]
Dreyfus et al., [9] describing the growth of the Denver neighborhood
health center program, wrote:

> As the program expanded . . . from one health center
> into a city-wide ambulatory care system, continuing ed-
> ucation of our physician staff became an important mo-
> tivating factor in recruiting and holding qualfied physicians.
> The staff grew to over 50 full-time and 20 part-time
> physicians who varied widely in age, place, and type
> of training and previous experience. Some came

directly from internships and residencies, others
from established research programs, still others
from private or hospital practice. They had no
common bond of medical experience, being for
the most part strangers to one another.

As the Denver program matured, these authors pointed out such
traditional accountability mechanisms as credentials, record review
and pharmacy committees were established.

The great emphasis placed on internal professional accountability
at the MLK Center is shown by the allocation of a large section of
their Sixth Annual Report to "Quality of Care."[10] Keeping in mind
that the MLK Center is one of the oldest and best established of the
NHCs and that their procedures may not be representative, it is
instructive nonetheless to review the elements of their approach. To
begin with, a new "problem-oriented record" was adopted to replace
the traditional, highly unsatisfactory methods of record keeping. Many
of the physicians showed a great deal of resistance to this change so
that adoption of the new system has been gradual. Second, a Medical
Care Evaluation Committee was established to evaluate the care of
families and to suggest improvement, but not to "police the activities
of practitioners." Third, a patient grievance procedure was established. This activity, to the present writer, transcends the Patient's
Bill of Rights of the American Hospital Association in its acceptance
of accountability to patients (see Appendix F). It is reproduced in
the hope that its spirit, if not its letter, will be replicated, not only
in NHCs but in all other health facilities.

A fourth component of the internal audit is an annual review of
all charts by the Family Health Worker. Another element is a review
of all of the charts of Nurse Practitioners by the Nursing Personnel
Supervisor and finally, a rarely encountered dental evaluation is
conducted by a dentist from another health center. It is not known how
well the total audit program actually works, but some results of external quality audits are presented below as an indication of the level
of health care provided in NHCs.

Internal Flow of Funds

In view of the newness of the NHC concept, of the various problems
associated with their establishment and of the difficulty of attracting
both professional and managerial personnel, it is not surprising to
find (as Sparer and Anderson did) that "a review of the fiscal, accounting and budget operations of the Neighborhood Health Centers during

late 1967 and early 1968 indicated that none were routinely collecting
cost data that would aid in the setting of a unit or per capita rate for
health-care services. Cost-finding methodology for ambulatory health
care had not been established, and cost analyses were rarely made."[11]
Besides the lack of available accounting techniques and of experienced
financial controllers was the important, perhaps overriding consideration that "a substantial problem in the financial management of the
centers has been that their funding through project grants built in no
incentives for efficiency."[12] (One is reminded here of the analagous
absence of incentives under the cost-plus reimbursement techniques
still prevalent in many hospital settings.)

It was not until some five or six years after the program com-
menced that the Office of Economic Opportunity issued guidelines for
cost finding in NHCs.[13] Documentation of the relative lack of internal
financial controls was provided by a General Accounting Office report
which noted that "the lack of reliable data hampered GAO at all NHCs
visited," and that "GAO noted inefficient administrative and operating
practices within the NHCs."[14] Under the pressures by Congress of
becoming self-sufficient units, NHCs have been forced to tighten up
their whole financial structure. Special attention is now being paid
to receiving increased revenues from Medicare, Medicaid and other
third party payers and, looking further down the line, many NHCs
are undertaking feasibility studies to determine the best approaches
for achieving Health Maintenance Organization status.

The internal reaction to these pressures may be examplified
again, by citing the MLK Center's Sixth Report:[15]

> The Center has, for the first time, hired an accountant
> to fill the position of comptroller. Prior to this, the
> Center had to depend on Montefiore Hospital for doing
> the accounting and providing financial data. The role
> of the comptroller will be more important in the event
> Montefiore is no longer the grantee and no longer
> provides us with these services.

And further;

> The comptroller reports to the administration of the
> Center. He sees to it that the above areas are function-
> ing at the highest level. He makes sure that financial
> information is recorded and forwarded to the proper
> agencies. He checks items of expenditures for ap-
> propriateness and budget approval. He informs the
> administration as to financial status on a monthly
> basis or as requested. He is involved in the Center

Information system as to the financial data. Internal
reports and systems for finance are prepared and submitted to the administration from above departments
(Payroll, Accounting, Billing) through the Comptroller's office.

As is well known, the gap between description and reality is a
wide one, but the outline itself of the functions necessary for internal
financial management is indicative of an all-out attack on the problems
raised by the GAO. Comparisons in financial terms of the cost of
health services provided by NHCs and those provided in other settings
will be deferred to a later section of the chapter.

EXTERNAL ACCOUNTABILITY

Legal and Governance

Some of the external legal problems that NHCs are involved with
are discussed in another section of the MLK's Sixth Report under the
heading of "Health Law."[16] Many of their legal problems are not
unique to the New York City situation and bear mention here. To
illustrate: All attorneys of NHCs are concerned with such problems
as involuntary commitment of NHC patients to mental institutions;
utilization of the emergency room; conflict of interest between patients
and consent of minors to medical treatment.
    A second area concerns changes in health law that have a specific
bearing on NHC operations such as the expanded use of paraprofes-
sionals, licensing, and Medicaid eligibility.
    A third area of particular interest to the community orientation
of NHCs is the training of Health Advocates of the (MLKs) Department
of Community Health Advocacy.
    A fourth area of large legal involvement concerns the transforma-
tion of NHCs into HMOs, with the attendant problems of legal organizational forms and of insurance regulations.
    We mentioned, in passing, some of the governance problems of
NHCs. The MLK Center unfortunately, is a good case in point. One
of the major reasons for the delay in transferring control of the institution from Montefiore Hospital, the present grantee, to the Community Board was the conflict between between black and Puerto
Rican board members. Blacks disputed a November 1971 election
which resulted in a preponderance of Puerto Rican board members.
As one Washington official of OEO stated, "When the Government

puts [in] large programs on the basis that the community will participate, that clearly becomes an important activity, and there is going
to be competition for control."[17] The same official noted that there
were similar struggles for control between blacks and Spanish-speaking
people in Los Angeles, Denver, Chicago, San Francisco, and Brooklyn.
Paradoxically, community control of NHCs which was seen as a means
of expanding health services becomes, in instances such as those
mentioned, a divisive force which posed a severe challenge to con-
tinuance of the governance structure as originally perceived.

Quality and Functional Accountability

An innovative type of health service in an existing health care
system that is not famous for structural experimentation is bound to
develop rather quickly two polarized groups of critics—those who are
vociferous proponents of the change, and traditionalists who insist
that the highest standards set by the grade A medical school-affiliated
hospitals or the highly skilled specialists in the office represent the
only acceptable quality level. It must be admitted that the bulk of the
writing on the NHCs has been done by proponents, and much of it is
couched in general, laudatory terms.

One of the more noteworthy attempts at objective assessment of
the quality of care provided by NHCs is the study by Morehead et al.,[18]
who comprised an evaluation unit of the Department of Community
Health at the Albert Einstein College of Medicine. The study was
originally published in the American Journal of Public Health in 1971
and has since been included in the collection of articles entitled
Neighborhood Health Centers to which we have already referred. The
Morehead study utilized a "baseline medical audit" of 35 OEO NHCs
and compared the quality of care so measured against the quality
provided in medical school outpatient departments. With the average
score of three specialties in the latter setting set at 100, the study
found that OEO Centers had an overall average of 107 and that they
exceeded the medical school affiliated outpatient department in the
subclasses of medicine (112 vs. 94) and in pediatrics (190 vs. 83),
but not in obstetrics (121 vs. 124). The OEO Centers also showed a
higher overall average than "group practices" (107 vs. 103) and exceeded the latter in medicine (112 vs. 102) and pediatrics (90 vs. 84)
and were almost on a par in obstetrics (121 vs. 122).[19] In sum,[20]

> The conclusion reached from review of this data is that
> at the present time, with the exception of the few small,
> highly organized and richly staffed Children's Bureau
> programs, the neighborhood health center program

performance is generally equal to and in some instances superior to that of other established pro-
vidors of health care.

Another study of 21 of the older NHCs, commissioned by the
Office of Planning, Research, and Evaluation of the OEO, was published in 1972 by Geomet, Incorporated. [21] This study had a somewhat broader focus than the Morehead one (Mildred Morehead, incidentally, was a consultant here) in that its objective was to indicate
the extent "to which the NHCs are achieving their basic objective of
providing comprehensive care to a community"[22]—functional accountability in our terms. The study's conclusions may perhaps best be
summed up by paraphrasing its "objectives" and "results."
   First, in answer to the question of how well the NHCs were
reaching the target population, the study group found that on average
the Centers reached about two-thirds of those eligible with three-
quarters of those reached considering the Center as their usual source
of care. Second, with respect to patient satisfaction, the study found
that patients generally spoke well of the Center, but so did nonusers
of their own sources of care. The third objective—that of assessing
the degree to which the NHCs were fulfilling their overall mission of
providing adequate care—the study found that while generally the
Centers were providing a wide range of services, the larger centers
scored higher on "appropriate utilization and comprehensiveness,"
whereas the smaller centers performed relatively better in the area
of continuity, family orientation, and patient satisfaction. Deficiencies
in mental health services were noted in the overall program. On the
fourth objective, that of relating structure to performance, Geomet
found that the superior performers were "those which serve fewer
active registrants but spend more on each, which have achieved
stability and which stress community involvement and outreach as part
of their operations." The last objective of the study was not evaluatory,
concerning itself instead with feasibility of developing a methodology
for measuring the antipoverty impact of NHCs.
   Conclusions based on two studies, even apparently good ones
such as the Morehead on quality and the Geomet on function—are obviously quite tentative. When combined with the general tenor of other
literature on NHCs, we are inclined to go along with the proponents
in believing that the NHCs are delivering, with a large modicum of public accountability, relatively high levels of appropriate health care.

Fiscal and Cost Accountability

Unfortunately, no convenient single source of data on NHCs—all
of which are now funded by HEW—is presently available. [23] An early

estimate by Daniel I. Zwick indicated that between 1965 and 1971 over $400 million had been spent for NHCs and other local projects. [24] As indicated earlier, the General Accounting Office found many deficiencies in the fiscal reporting systems of many NHCs.

The Geomet study found that in the "high performing centers" the cost of care averaged $250 annually per registrant, while in the remaining ten in their study the average cost was $150 per registrant, with an annual average cost for active registrant for the 21 centers of approximately $200.25.[25] The annual budget of the MLK Center discussed earlier was roughly $8 1/2 million, which when averaged over the 39,000 "individuals in households registered and receiving care" gives an annual cost for registrant of about $218.[26] Ginzberg et al.[27] raised some questions with regard to such costs:

> Annual costs of about $250 per person, exclusive of hospitalization, have been encountered at some centers in New York City offering a broad spectrum of services. To provide care for all the nation's poor at such a rate would require a magnitude of expenditures which the federal budget cannot reasonably be expected to absorb.

On the other hand, Sparer and Anderson in a two-year cost study found that the costs of NHC visits compared favorably with those in the outpatient departments of hospitals. In their view, "From the standpoint of the quality of services, volume and use of services and costs, the Neighborhood Health Center is viable and cost efficient as compared with other providers."[28] Robertson et al.[29] take issue with the crude estimate of the previous study. The upshot of these cost analyses is that there are still no national or state standards for cost-finding, and that each investigator includes in average cost those elements best designed to prove some previously held contention concerning the functions of the NHCs.

With federal grant money decreasing and with NHCs being made increasingly dependent on Medicare, Medicaid, and other insurance payments and with plans afoot for transformation into HMOs (with attendant requirement for determining capitation fees) pressures to adopt uniform financial reports are growing.

What should be borne in mind is that the type of comprehensive care provided by NHCs is not replicated elsewhere and that, understandably, costs will be higher. This is not to deny the need for stricter financial controls, for the promotion of efficiency and for the search for optimum facility size. Moreover, the cost studies alluded to were all undertaken some five years after the commencement of the program so that inordinately high start-up costs were encountered. One physician associated with the El Rio-Santa Cruz Neighborhood Center in Tucson, Arizona, noted:[30]

It's true we are spending $1.2 million per year for
10,000 people or $120 per person. There are two points
to be made, however: First, the additional services
include all consulting services, psychiatry, social
services, nutritionist and health educator, a full
pharmacy at no extra charge: everything in fact
except dental care and the payment of hospital bills.
Also included in the cost are a transportation system,
an extensive training and job program for the unem-
ployed, plus research and evaluation including computerized data collection. Moreover, such Centers
always run into a tremendous backlog of unmet health
needs in an underprivileged area.

The second point on costs is that similar programs
have been shown to decrease hospital utilization, which
will help contain costs in the future.

Interfacility Cooperation

In one of their Guidance Memoranda, the OEO stated that the
professional aspects of an NHC must be such to assure high quality
standards and that "if such competence is not available the organizing
group . . . must make necessary arrangements with a qualified health
organization."[31] From the outset then, NHCs were not seen as independent entities but as part of the network of existing health facilities.
Neighborhood Health Centers are affiliated for the most part with
medical schools and teaching and community hospitals but they may
also be associated with group practices and public health departments.
It is, of course, of the essence of the comprehensive care concept
that there exist a "back-up" hospital facility for patients who may
require hospitalization. Utilization of existing health organizations
and facilities also lessens the drain on the financial resources of the
Centers themselves.

One of the policy questions in the evaluation of NHCs by the OEO
was, in fact, that of coordination—coordination with other community
health providers and with back-up service. The extent of coordination
was measured by such variables as record transfers, referrals to the
Center, joint meetings, and personal and telephone consultations.
The Geomet study found coordination with state mental hospitals and
with local health and welfare departments to be high. The degree of
back-up services coordination appeared to be a function of the distance
between the NHC and the hospital as well as with the question of staff
privileges extended to NHC physicians.[32]

Hollister, Kramer, and Bellin[33] maintain that hospitals are motivated by self-interest in their relationships with NHCs. "The neighborhood centers," they state, "are no longer valued for their potential to decrease hospitalization, but are seen as new sources of patients to fill empty hospital beds. Hospitals are now interested in serving as back-ups to the neighborhood units partly because the centers provide an additional pool of patients with third party payers attached." The implication here is that if hospitals were experiencing high occupancy rates, the degree of cooperation between them and NHCs would be diminished. Such an hypothesis is beyond the scope of this study to investigate, and can be tested only by selecting high occupancy rate hospitals and measuring the degree of coordination between them and NHCs.

What should be recognized is that the NHCs do pose a "threat" to hospital outpatient departments, perhaps, in some cases, sufficient to cause the hospitals to eliminate their OPDs. This is an issue which cannot, however, be decided on a priori bases but rather on a careful, case by case analysis of the health impact on a community of varying modes of providing comprehensive ambulatory services.

Consumer Accountability

As has been repeatedly stressed, consumer participation in the organization and administration of NHCs was one of the pillars of the OEO enabling legislation in the "Healthright" projects. Whereas in other health institutions, consumer participation is minimal, or may be incidental to the organization's operation, in the NHCs it is built in and may be viewed as one of the raisons d'etre of the facility. Hochbaum, [34] in a perceptive article, noted that "as is the fate of many such newly discovered concepts, it (consumer participation) is being greeted with attitudes ranging from total rejection and dubious caution to overoptimistic enthusiasm, and is embraced by some as though it were a poisonous snake, by others as though it heralded an era of social harmony and of perfect health services for all."

Previously we noted that many NHC boards and advisory councils were, (and are) the scenes of internal conflict, not only between the several groups involved (board, hospital, and the like) but intragroup tensions prevailed as well. Zwick[35] has pointed out that "Critics have frequently not been as tolerant of error in these cases as in more established institutions." Hochbaum, who is somewhat more cautious and less sanguine about the role of consumers than Zwick, argued cogently that[36]

. . . quite plausible claims for greater utilization of
health services following consumer participation in
the planning of such services have been made in
several instances. Yet I know of no really convinc-
ing or even persuasive evidence that such consumer
participation is resulting in health services which
are any better and more effective than health services that are planned by professionals who make a
concerted effort to learn about, understand and
appreciate the characteristics and needs of the
people to be served. In fact, I suspect that often
the opposite is true. Joint planning by consumers
and providers can easily lead to compromises between conflicting opinions, to dilution of standards
and thereby to <u>less</u> adequate services.

CONCLUSION

Neighborhood Health Centers were, unfortunately, mandated to
pursue many and often conflicting goals. (The employment of local
residents, for example, may not always produce high quality services
at minimum cost.)[37] The most important function of NHCs, in the
present writer's view, was (and is) that of filling a serious gap in the
existing health system—mainly, the provision of relatively comprehensive, easily accessible, low-cost ambulatory care services. This is
no easy task, in and of itself, and it was further complicated by the
community participatory nature of the governance structure. These
factors, together with simple growing pains and the more subtle opposition of medical organizations and facilities generated inevitable
conflicts that, in turn, detracted from the optimal functioning of
NHCs. Nonetheless, the general experience has been, on the whole,
praiseworthy.

Unlike many of the other health facilities reviewed in earlier
chapters, accountability occupies a central role in the thinking and
practice of NHCs, a role which unfortunately has not always been
fulfilled. The recruitment of experienced managerial personnel and
of high quality professionals will remain stubborn problems. NHCs
present a most interesting testing ground of the extent to which
heightened accountability to consumers for quality and to the funding
sources for efficient use of resources, will produce a viable and
innovative mode of health organization.

1. Eli Ginzberg et al., <u>Urban Health Services: The Case of New York</u> (New York: Columbia University Press, 1971), p. 136.

2. Daniel I. Zwick, Some Accomplishments and Findings of Neighborhood Health Centers," in Robert M. Hollister, Bernard M. Kramer, and Seymour S. Bellin, Neighborhood Health Centers (Boston: Lexington Books [D. C. Heath and Co.], 1974), p. 72.

3. Guidance, Healthright Programs, OEO Guidance No. 6128-1, March 1970, p. 2.

4. Ibid., p. 6.

5. Martin Luther King Jr. Health Center, <u>The Sixth Report</u>, (January 1972—July 1973), p. 6.

6. Ann Stokes, David Banta, and Samuel Putnam, "The Columbia Point Health Association: Evolution of a Community Health Board," <u>American Journal of Public Health</u> 62, no. 9 (September 1972), and Milton S. Davis and Robert E. Tranguada, "A Sociological Evaluation of the Watts Neighborhood Health Center," <u>Medical Care</u> 7, no. 2 (March-April 1969).

7. New York <u>Times</u>.

8. Harold Wise, "The Primary-Care Health Team," <u>Archives of Internal Medicine</u> 130 (September 1972), p. 443.

9. Edward G. Dreyfus, Ronald Munson, John A. Sbarboro, and David L. Cowen, "Internal Chart Audits in a Neighborhood Health Program," <u>Medical Care</u> 9, no. 5 (September-October 1971), p. 450.

10. Martin Luther King Jr. Health Center, op. cit., p. 178ff.; see also note 9.

11. Gerald Sparer and Arne Anderson, "Cost of Services at Neighborhood Health Centers—A Comparative Analysis," in Hollister et al., op. cit., p. 180. For alternative cost calculations see Robert C. Robertson, Gordon T. Moore, Irene Butler, and Elisabeth Hall, "Costs and Financing Policies at a Neighborhood Health Center," <u>Inquiry</u> 10, no. 3 (September 1973), pp. 36–48.

12. Hollister et al., op. cit., p. 177.

13. Sparer and Anderson, op. cit., pp. 180-181 and references 5-6, p. 188.

14. "Implementation of a Policy of Self-Support by Neighborhood Health Centers," Report to the Subcommittee on Health, Committee on Labor and Public Welfare, United States Senate, Office of the Comptroller General of the United States, May 1973, pp. 1—2.

15. Martin Luther King Jr. Health Center, op. cit., p. 227.

16. Ibid., p. 318ff.

17. New York <u>Times</u>, January 12, 1972.

18. Mildred A. Morehead, Rose S. Donaldson, and Mary R. Seravalli, "Comparison Between OEO Neighborhood Health Centers and Other Health Care Providers of Ratings of the Quality of Health Care," in Hollister et al., op. cit., pp. 257-273. For a more detailed discussion of methodology, see Mildred A. Morehead, "Evaluating Quality of Medical Care in the Neighborhood Health Center Program of the Office of Economic Opportunity," Medical Care 8, no. 2 (March-April 1970).

19. Ibid., p. 262.

20. Ibid., p. 272

21. "Study to Evaluate the OEO Neighborhood Health Center Program at Selected Centers," Volume 1, Final Report, Geomet Report Number H.E. 71, Geomet, Inc., Rockville, Md., January 1972.

22. Ibid., p. iii.

23. A national reporting system including all 118 Neighborhood Centers and 39 Family Centers will become operational during fiscal year 1975. Personal communication to author from Department of Health, Education, and Welfare dated May 29, 1974.

24. Zwick, op. cit., p. 71.

25. Geomet Report, op. cit., pp. 37-38.

26. Martin Luther King Jr. Health Center, op. cit., pp. 28-29.

27. Urban Health Services, op. cit., p. 154.

28. Sparer and Anderson, op. cit., p. 187.

29. Robertson et al., op. cit., note 17, p. 147.

30. Peter D. Mott, "Comments," in Arizona Medicine 28, no. 4 (April 1971), pp. 313-314.

31. Guidance, Healthright Programs, op. cit., p. 6.

32. Geomet Report, op. cit., pp. 120-123, p. 161.

33. Hollister, et al., op. cit., p. 17.

34. G. M. Hochbaum, "Consumer Participation in Health Planning: Toward Conceptual Clarification," American Journal of Public Health 59, no. 9 (September 1969), p. 1698.

35. Zwick, op. cit., p. 76.

36. Hochbaum, op. cit., p. 1702. Emphasis in original.

37. See for example Lowell Eliezer Bellin, "The New Left and American Public Health—Attempted Radicalization of the A.P.H.A. Through Dialectic," American Journal of Public Health 60, no. 6 (June 1970), p. 977.

6

IMPROVING
MECHANISMS FOR
ACCOUNTABILITY

This final chapter has two objectives: the first is to pinpoint some weak links in the existing structure of accountability and the second is to discuss some new proposals for enhancing the accountability process, both in the types of facilities discussed previously as well as in the health care system generally.

A pervasive problem surrounding the ensuing discussion is the fact that health, like education, has traditionally been a state function. The infusion of large amounts of money into health care from the federal government, accompanied by new strictures on the use of those funds, has resulted in jurisdictional overlapping and diffusion— leading in turn to ambiguity concerning the locus of responsibility as well as of accountability. Little will come from the following suggestions until these intergovernmental problems can be rectified.

THE VOLUNTARY HOSPITALS

In a well-known, six-part series exposing extensive conflict-of-interest transactions involving "10 of the 38 current trustees" of the Washington D. C. Hospital Center, Ronald Kessler of the Washington Post revealed, among other things;[1]

> Establishment by the hospital's treasurer of an interest-free account with balances frequently hovering around $1 million and ranging up to $1.8 million at a bank where the treasurer was a vice president; funneling of stock brokerage business of the hospital's investment committee to the

> son-in-law of a trustee . . . formation by the
> hospital's administrators of a company whose
> first contract, amounting to $616,000 last year,
> was awarded, without competitive bidding, on
> approval by the hospital's board of trustees.

The Temporary State Commission on Living Costs and the Economy
(N. Y.) has revealed other instances of apparent trustee improprieties
and has pointed out that "presently, the law does not prohibit hospital
trustees from doing business with the hospital they serve. There are
no requirements for open bidding, disqualification of trustees as
vendors or scrutiny of the contracting process by any other outside
agency."[2]

Since trustees do occupy commanding and sensitive positions in
the hospital hierarchy, it would appear that remedial action is required along several fronts. First, state law should prescribe that
trustees or their relatives be prohibited from doing business with
the hospital, or, at the very least, that complete public disclosure
of any and all dealings must be made. Enforcement of this kind of
provision requires the filing of certified affidavits with heavy penalties
for fraud. Second, new procedures for election to boards should be
promulgated (likewise by the state) with measures to insure representation by noninterested parties who reside in the hospital's catchment
area. Third, meetings of the trustees or boards should be open to
the public—as was recently announced by the Board of Managers of
the Nassau County Medical Center.[3]

Beyond these matters of board composition is the basic question
of board function. The American College of Hospital Administrators,
in a seminar on medical staff law, put the matter plainly:[4]

> Perhaps the most important duty and the one least
> attended to is the duty that the board provide satis-
> factory patient care. It is only through the fulfill-
> ment of this duty that the basic purpose of the
> hospital will be accomplished. The elements of
> this duty are varied and extend from the purchase
> of the most suitable equipment and machines for
> patient care to the hiring of a competent admin-
> istrator and other employees and selection and
> general supervision of competent physicians. Thus,
> one of the most important duties and one that is
> generally not fully obeyed is that of setting stand-
> ards and regulations for evaluating the provision
> of medical care in the institution.

The implementation of a charge such as this requires a body with a wide variety of expertise and one that is unlikely to exist anywhere. A rethinking of the current board arrangement is obviously required. To begin with, the chief administrator and head of the medical staff should be key members of any board. Possibly the creation of a separate technical advisory board operating essentially at the same level of existing boards may be appropriate. Similarly, the links between existing boards and Community Advisory Boards should be strengthened by more frequent contacts and a greater delegation of powers to the latter. The Governing Board, by broadening its network of inputs, will be acting with the advantage of greater intelligence and, at the same time, will be acting in a manner designed to gain community-wide acceptance.

Democratizing the board and infusing it with greater intelligence are but the beginnings of the proper reconstruction of the governance mechanism. The all-important, day-to-day management of the hospital is in the hands of the Administrator, who can either implement good general policy or who, whether by ignorance or design, may impede its execution. Through the exercise of creative leadership, the Administrator may, almost as an independent force, guide the hospital along optimal paths. Etzioni[5] has indicated the appropriate strategy here:

> The object is not to fly in the face of reality or power groups, nor to wildly pursue utopian notions of social justice or accountability—such an administrator is all too likely to be quickly expelled—but to help shape, mobilize and combine the vectors which determine the health unit's direction and accountability model so as to bring them closer to the desired system.

Let us turn next to the thorny question of the quality of care provided by the voluntary hospital. In the first chapter and at various other points in this essay we discussed the role of the Joint Commission on the Accreditation of Hospitals in standard setting via periodic surveys and hospital accreditation. The movement from a completely voluntary to a quasi-legal institution has strengthened JCAH but weaknesses persist in the areas of the scope of its concerns, the lack of qualified personnel, provision for consumer input, and the frequency and publicity of its audit activities. These faults are remediable given the necessary motivation, funds, and time.

Acceptability of JCAH by the health professions generally is an attribute, the importance of which should not be minimized. *

Almost as if to fill some of the functional gaps in JCAH, Congress passed the Professional Standards Review Organization Act (P. L. 92-603) as part of the 1972 Social Security Amendments, which was designed to monitor and evaluate the care, treatment, and costs for patients covered by the Medicare and Medicaid acts. PSROs embody the concept of peer review and have won the (belated) endorsement of the American Medical Association as well as that of the American Hospital Association. In what must have been an unguarded moment, one AMA official stated, "We have demonstrated to the public that we are willing [sic] to enter into an agreement with the government to be accountable for tax funds."[6]

The PSRO concept embodies a variety of regulatory techniques and mechanisms: (following Abel-Smith's typology[7]) persuasive regulation as represented by the notion of peer review; punitive regulation in the provision for fines; postevent regulation represented by comparisons of predetermined norms (for example, "excessive" hospitalization); prior approval regulation for hospital admissions and a generalized attempt at cost controls. Despite, or perhaps because of its ambitious program, PSROs have been criticized on a number of grounds. Etzioni has questioned the propriety of the norm-setting procedure, the efficacy of the economic sanctions (up to $5,000 in fines), and the objectivity of a situation that allows "the guards . . . to guard the guardians."[8] As an alternative, Etzioni proposed a Comprehensive Health Audit to be performed periodically be specialized, independent, government certified auditing corporations that would overcome the deficiencies inherent in the PSRO legislation as it now stands.

----

*On the other hand, a rather disquieting report issued recently by the Department of Health, Education, and Welfare, may compel us to reevaluate JCAH's procedures and overall effectiveness, as well as Titles 18 and 19 themselves. Acting in accord with a 1972 amendment to Titles 18 and 19 that permits the federal government to spot check JCAH, HEW found that 66 percent of a national sample of hospitals had "significant health and safety deficiencies." Despite findings of inadequate fire safeguards, improper drug records, inadequate nursing staff, lack of control in dietary departments and other violations, no penalties were applied and there was no reduction in federal payments to the hospitals. The section chief of hospitals of HEW stated, "There is nothing in the law that would allow us to reduce payments." (New York _Times_, March 23, 1975, p. 45.)

Another mechanism designed to secure external accountability which was discussed above is certificate-of-need legislation. Leveson[9] has pointed to a number of serious weaknesses in this device, among which are

(a) The C-O-N device is not an effective cost control mechanism since services rendered per bed are more important than bed numbers.

(b) There may be overutilization of beds now.

(c) No consensus exists as to criteria for determining optimal bed numbers.

(d) Need for beds is decided mainly on effective demand criterion.

(e) The C-O-N agency may be dominated by hospital industry.

(f) C-O-N agency not effective in closing marginal facilities.

(g) C-O-N actions by controlling supply would require price controls to prevent resulting potential price increases.

Added to these is the more general point raised by Abel-Smith that "It is not enough . . . to be able to refuse permission without having any authority to initiate action either to build more beds when they are needed or to develop alternative patterns of care that would make more beds unnecessary."[10] These criticisms, while well taken, suffer from an all-or-nothing kind of thinking—they fail to consider the alternative of no legislation or of the possibilities for enlarging the scope and improving the operation of existing legislation. The fact that C-O-N legislation doesn't do everything, or doesn't do perfectly what it is supposed to do, is not sufficient basis for rejecting it. The present writer holds with the more balanced view of Anne Somers,[11] which while based specifically on New Jersey's experience, nonetheless has wider applicability:

Assuming this transition from an unplanned health care economy, which was not working, to a planned economy, which has yet to prove itself was necessary—an assumption upon which this paper is predicated—the success of the regulatory approach may depend on its ability to assimilate entrepreneurial initiative and professional expertise and to combine these values with public accountability—and effective administration.

One of the weakest (because one of the most complex) yet most visible links in the accountability network is that of cost containment. A New York State cost-of-living commission pointed out, for example, that in 1963 the average hospital stay in New York State cost $426;

in 1973 that figure rose to $1, 325. 51. [12] Hospital administrators will
lay the blame for escalating costs to wages and salaries to a lack of
cost-consciousness among physicians who order tests and X-rays,
to an unconcern with productivity among all personnel, to the high
cost of equipment and supplies and high borrowing rates. The ease
with which high costs are passed on to the patient has been laid at the
door of the reimbursement mechanism. External critics emphasize
poor management in general as a contributing factor. There is, of
course, truth in each of these allegations. I have elsewhere examined
some of the ways in which intra- and interhospital efficiency may be
increased and will not reexplore that territory here. [13]

Some of the points discussed earlier in the chapter such as PSROs,
the role of the administrator, the role of the trustees, and certificate-
of-need legislation, are aimed directly or indirectly at containing
costs. Since so large a portion of hospital revenues are now derived
from third-party payers, these payers (Medicare and Medicaid, the
"blues," and commercial carriers) stand at critical junctures in the
flow-of-funds system. The government has already begun the process
of attempting to clamp down through the PSROs and only recently,
Blue Cross has likewise begun the process of applying pressure at
nodal points. Walter McNerney, president of the Blue Cross Association, in a statement which to many health analysts was long overdue,
remarked, "The Blue Cross System feels strongly that it must be
more than a conduit for subscribers' money, more than a payer of
bills. "[14] The new program which the national Blue Cross Association
asked all of its members to institute includes, among other things,
setting up a Blue Cross utilization review mechanism; the encouragement of alternatives to inpatient care; prospective as opposed to retrospective reimbursement formulas; cooperation with Comprehensive
Health Planning agencies, particularly in the area of certificate of need
implementation; encouragement of individual plans to convert to Health
Maintenance Organizations; to increase public accountability to its 117
million subscribers by reconstituting governing boards to make certain
that most members represent the public, rather than the health professions, and the encouragement of computer technology to effect increases in efficiency. [15] It appears to this writer that what remains
to be done is to consolidate governmental, Blue Cross, and state
legislative cost control activities, perhaps by means of local cost
control and rate-setting boards, and to mandate open hearings with
full disclosure of data and decisions to the public-at-large.

This brings us to a discussion of the apex of the accountability
network vis-a-vis the voluntary hospital—namely the role of the consumer. Hortatory slogans and global rhetoric abound in this area,
to wit:[16]

The power of the consumer to control and influence the
delivery system must be exercised at every level of the
health care system: facility, service system or program
and neighborhood, city, state, region or nation. This
power should include but not be limited to making policy,
controlling assets (including capital expenditures), facilities, equipment and services.

Diametrically opposed to this view is that of a hospital administrator, who maintains that "To put the power of decision over the
expenditure of millions of dollars and thousands of employees in the
hands of those without the necessary education and experience is
certainly not in the best interest of the community;" and adds, "It is
important to remember . . . that sensitivity to the desires and needs
of the community is not equivalent to offering control to any except
those most capable of exercising control."[17]

A Medicaid task force recommended that "any federally funded
and/or operated health programs must provide for consumer participants on advisory committees and councils concerned with planning,
purchasing and delivering health services."[18] In the same view, the
group urged "majority representation of consumers and consumer
representatives" on State Medicaid Advisory Committees, and also
that proprietary facilities "should be encouraged to provide for consumer involvement in the monitoring of their services."[19] It is one
thing, however, to urge and even to mandate consumer participation,
but quite another to implement it. Edward Sparer puts his finger on
one of the major problems in this area. "What is lacking in provider
institutions," he maintains, " . . . is any real sense of commitment
to consumerism. What is lacking, by and large, is a willingness to
break with professionalist philosophy. As a result, except where outside pressure has forced activity, providers are usually unwilling to
engage in serious consumer constituency building efforts."[20] One
manifestation of provider reticence is the fact that even when consumers
are represented there is "a failure to participate in decisional rather
than advisory functions."[21] This failure, it should be noted, may be
attributed in part to consumer deficiencies as well. For example,
an American Friends Service Committee report on a project to evaluate
consumer participation in health planning, cited a number of "barriers
to effective consumer participation in health planning or administration." Among these were the fact that for low-income consumers
especially, long-range planning in medicine is not a "top priority"
since they view health care as crisis medicine. Moreover, as the
study indicated, consumers are unfamiliar with complex laws, regulations, and technical material. Then too there is the potential for
cooptation, as illustrated by the following story:[22]

In Houston, leaders in the fight to establish community health services and clinics surrendered their
advocacy roles and their community leadership when
offered jobs in the clinic or its related programs. In
fact, some sought or appointed themselves to the very
jobs they had helped to create by their leadership. And,
being economically dependent upon their jobs and new to
them, they were fearful of continuing to criticize or to
participate in efforts to improve the system or services.

Even though the consumer movement in health is barely emerging,
reports such as the one just cited and others have engendered, in
some, a feeling of frustration and disillusionment. As Wellington
and Tischler expressed it, "Experience with both professional social
activism and the professional oversell give rise to the suspicion in
both blue-collar white and ghetto black communities that community
participation, today's royal road to romance, is really just an updated
primrose path."[23]
Nonetheless, despite these disappointments, and others that are
sure to come, consumer participation in health decisions, whether
because it is required by legislation or because of demands by consumer
groups (or those who purport to speak on their behalf), is a movement
which is present and growing. A most important impetus to consumerism comes from administrators themselves. Peter Terenzio, an experienced and knowledgeable administrator, put the matter in terms
of enlightened self-interest: "If we in the urban hospitals fail to
recognize and act on this realization [namely, responsiveness to the
community] we may find that instead of working "with the community"
we may be working "for the community."[24]
One aspect of working with the community is the provision of
health education to consumers in order to improve their knowledge of
the health delivery system, thus enabling them to provide informed
inputs either to hospital governing boards or to their own groups. To
this end the American Hospital Association has recommended the
establishment of a national clearinghouse for consumer health education.[25] From the consumer side of the picture, a new organization
was formed several years ago in New York—the Consumer Commission on the Accreditation of Health Services—for the purpose of providing consumers with factual data on the cost and quality of health
services. In the words of the Commission, "We believe that individual
consumers, as well as large purchasers of health services in New
York, must have a voice in the evaluation and delivery of routine and
critical life-saving services. The full disclosure of factual data on
health services, particularly hospitals, can lead to more intelligent
use of the system by consumers." And further, "It is extremely

important for the health consumer to know that he is in a position to negotiate for the health services he needs rather than be overwhelmed by the vast and complex health establishment in New York."26 In all probability, groups similar to CCAHS will emerge in other areas as well. *

Within the hospital itself, we have seen the recent establishment of ombudsmen or patient advocates whose task it is to determine whether the consumer-patient is satisfied with the care received, and, if not, to funnel the complaints to the proper authorities. Such personnel, because of their intimate knowledge of what goes on in the hospital, can be vital links in the accountability structure. Not only can they render the actual patient less helpless in a complex bureaucratic setting, but they can also provide valuable inputs to consumer groups at large, especially in the area of the quality of care provided—potential versus actual. Every health care facility should be mandated to have patient advocates (in some proportion to its bed size) and the source of income of such personnel should be other than the facility itself. Needless to say, an educational training program for such personnel, given by competent and objective professionals and carried on in separate educational settings, is an essential ingredient for an effective program in this area.

What is needed, finally, to round out the voluntary hospital accountability web is a quantitative and qualitative upgrading of state and local Comprehensive Health Planning Agencies, including legislative amendments to transform advisory functions into mandatory rules and regulations with effective economic and professional sanctions built in.

VA HOSPITALS

The political power inherent in the special constituency of VA hospitals—veterans of the U.S. Armed Forces—was demonstrated in the resignation recently of the Administrator of Veterans Affairs, an event to which we referred in Chapter 2. There are both positive and negative aspects to this exercise of "patient power." On the one hand, the resignation of the top official is an ultimate act of and concession to public accountability; on the other, it is a demonstration of the

---

*An excellent attempt at consumer education is the "Consumer's Guide to the Best Health Care For Your Money," reproduced in Appendix F.

potential superior influence of political over health considerations. There would appear to be lessons here for those who advocate complete governmental control over the health system.

As pointed out in Chapter 2, many of the problems of VA hospitals concern accountability of Congress and the President to the electorate in terms of adequate funding for VA and other federal hospitals. It was pointed out too that certain weaknesses remain in the area of accountability to younger veterans whose views and special needs are not given full weight in existing veterans' organizations.

In a recent report[27] to the Congress asking for budgetary increases, the VA stressed the following problems regarding its hospitals: Difficulty in recruiting doctors, nurses, and other staff members because of lower pay than that offered by private hospitals or private practice; limited numbers of surgeons who can provide such specialized skills as caring for paraplegics; a shortage of space and adequate equipment resulting in overcrowding and reduced standards of care and complex eligibility standards that confuse veterans. While increased appropriations may erase many of the problems cited, they will not serve to erase all. (Conspicuously absent from the list of problems were the medical and administrative complexities associated with the treatment of alcoholism and drug abuse—illnesses that affected a disproportionate number of Vietnam veterans.) VA hospitals, like their counterparts in the voluntary sector, appear to slight outpatient care and such supportive services as those of social workers, home health care, vocational counseling, and the like. It is in these areas that greater accountability for the kinds of care offered must be assumed by the VA hospitals.

STATE AND LOCAL HEALTH FACILITIES

As with VA hospitals, the operations of state and local health facilities are limited, primarily by budgetary constraints imposed by legislative committees and other governmental officials. Consequently, accountability for the functioning of such institutions becomes a political-fiscal issue between the electorate and those elected. Since funds for health facilities must compete with those for a variety of other important governmental functions, continuous open education of the electorate is necessary if the most appropriate allocative decisions are to be made.

Another important link in the accountability network in state and local facilities concerns the appointment of administrators and other high-level personnel. Historically, competent health professionals (M. D. s and others) have not been attracted to government service.

Competitive salaries and the ability of high-level administrators to exercise meaningful control over the delivery of services   are two prerequisites for change in this area.

In addition to the problems of attracting the necessary personnel, another weak link in the state and local system is the bureaucratic maze that has evolved in the administrative areas. New York State, for instance, recently retained an independent management consulting firm to delve into questions of authority and responsibility in the top- and middle-management echelons of the Department of Mental Hygiene— an agency which spends one billion dollars annually. [28] Such management reviews should be a permanent feature of governmental operations, particularly in the health field, where the consequences of mismanagement are not only higher costs but, as in the mental health area, withered lives.

In the earlier chapter on state and local facilities we noted the shift in power towards a consumer-oriented Task Force in the N. Y. State Department of Mental Hygiene. The scenario in that case followed, in part, Donald Ross' prescription to the effect that "Pressure generated through elected officials or an attempt to turn the quality of care into a campaign issue can sometimes change the make-up and policies of a public hospital."[29] This leaves open, however, the question of what to do in interelection periods.

Recent changes in financing, in particular those associated with Title 18 and 19, have served to raise the status of formerly indigent and medically indigent patients in state and local facilities, if not in the eyes of hospital personnel, then certainly in their own. This change in status to that of paying patients together with the quality and cost controls built into the legislation, as well as the growing consumer movement, [30] are important levers that are beginning to upgrade state and local facilities—traditionally low rankers by any measure of accountability.

PROPRIETARY HEALTH FACILITIES

Proprietary Hospitals

The data on hospital approvals and affiliations shown in Appendix A, Table A-2 point up the weak link in the already rather loose accountability structure in proprietary hospitals, namely, the relatively low JCAH accreditation ratio and the almost complete absence of seals of approval by other professional groups. As these hospitals begin to treat more patients who are covered by Medicare and Medicaid

or by a possibly new national health insurance mechanism, pressure
to upgrade quality will become more keenly felt so that the accreditation profile of proprietaries may, in time, begin to resemble that of
the voluntaries. However, so long as proprietary hospitals retain the
absolute right to select patients, certain kinds of approvals (for example, Council of Teaching Hospitals) will not be sought voluntarily.

A second weak link in the accountability network concerns the
extent of participation in Comprehensive Health Planning (314b)
Agencies. It is our view that such participation should be made mandatory on a nationwide basis for all health facilities. Finally, proprietary status should not be used as a shield behind which questionable
practices, whether financial, managerial or service-related, should
be perpetrated. There is a need for full disclosure of proprietary
hospitals' operations and for means of disseminating the relevant
aspects to health agencies and to consumers.

Nursing Homes

The recent four-part series of reports on nursing homes in The
New York Times[31] indicated that many of the deficiences that were
mentioned in Chapter 4 (and some new ones) continue to plague this
segment of health facilities. *

The largely proprietary nature of nursing homes has indeed en-
abled them to escape quality and financial surveillance by health
authorities. † The first order of business here is to render it mandatory that all nursing homes be brought under the supervision of the
health departments of all the states.

----

*As this is being written, Governor Carey has appointed a More-
land Act Commission to investigate nursing home abuses in New York
State and Senators Frank Church and Frank Moss and Representative
Edward Koch have introduced legislation calling for unified federal
action to deal with interstate linkages between nursing home scandals
and calling for the development of better cost controls consistent
with incentives for continuing good care. See New York Times, January 10, 1975 and Senate Special Committee on Aging, News, March
13, 1975. See also "Nursing Home Care in the United States: Failure
of Public Policy" Subcommittee on Long-Term Care of the Special
Committee on Aging, U.S. Senate, Committee Print, 94th Cong.,
1st Sess. (Supporting Papers 1-3 issued).

†In what was described as the first national study of nursing homes
by a governmental agency—the Department of Health, Education and
Welfare—in an interim report, "Long-Term Care Facility Improvement,"

Second, the health agencies should immediately set high minimum standards for the continued operation of nursing homes and, as a corollary, those same agencies must equip themselves with adequate means of enforcement of their regulations.

Third, since the great bulk of nursing home revenues are derived from Medicare and Medicaid, the implementing agencies must insist on high standards of quality and be in a position to carry out unannounced quality and financial audits to insure compliance.

The large and growing demand for extended care facilities in the face of a relatively inelastic supply renders the authorities reluctant to impose such severe penalties for fraud and malfeasance as decertification, license revocation, or the cutting off of funds. This situation has led to the suggestion by the Health Law Project of the University of Pennsylvania Law School that the legal remedy of receivership be utilized in this area. [32] Placing a nursing home under receivership would be an attempt to upgrade the quality of care without closing the facility. Needless to say, there are many legal as well as extralegal obstacles to the use of this device, but this kind of remedy should not be dismissed out of hand. Similarly, the suggestion from the same source that reimbursement rates should be tied to quality of care is worthy of consideration although one must be wary here of not denying funds to the poorer homes that will become poorer still. [33]

While not originating from the Pennsylvania Health Law Project, that group commented favorably on the creation of an Ombudsman Office as part of the state apparatus. Such an office and its field personnel would attempt to act on complaints by nursing home residents and would also perform an outreach function to keep apprised continuously of conditions of care. We have already endorsed the ombudsman concept in hospitals and believe that, given the nature of the patient population as well as the abuses that have been documented, an ombudsman function is even more imperative in the nursing home situation. [34]

One impediment to strengthening the accountability network that has recently surfaced in New York is the jurisdictional dispute between the state and city health departments concerning the locus of inspection authority in proprietary nursing homes and hospitals. [35]

---

indicated that "widespread deficiencies" were found in nursing homes, citing such problems of "overdrugging of patients, inadequate medical attention, inadequate diets, poor rehabilitation programs, and violations of federal regulations." (New York Times, April 2, 1975, p. 19.)

This problem arises from the equal shares (25 percent) contributed
for the Medicaid program by cities and states. Intergovernmental
problems of this kind should be resolved on the basis of which unit
is better equipped to perform the duties—as a general proposition in
this field, the closer the unit is to the facilities, the better able it
will be to perform its tasks—to monitor the situation and to implement
its decisions. This is especially true when, as in New York City
currently, the Health Commissioner does not shrink from "baring
his knuckles" before the health establishment. [36]

NEIGHBORHOOD HEALTH CENTERS

The basic question concerning NHCs is that having been launched,
can they remain in orbit? That they should remain viable health
providers is a strong bias of the present writer for reasons discussed
in Chapter 4.

The provisions for accountability written into the enabling legislation are far more extensive in the case of NHCs than they are for
any other type of health facility so far reviewed. Indeed, this may be
the Achilles heel of the program. For instance, the inability to attract
and to hold competent professional personnel may be traced to an unwillingness of professionals (given the nature of present medical education) to work under conditions of intense accountability-for-service.
In addition, as we have seen, consumer participation on a large scale
often results in internecine conflict, especially where the community
is ethnically polarized. Then too, the tendency for professional dominance on the part of the back-up hospital or medical school renders
ambivalent the questions of accountability—to whom and for what.

Financial and other pressures which are forcing NHCs to convert
to HMO status is in our view a mixed blessing. HMOs are based on
the concept of prepayment which, of necessity, requires the setting
of fees high enough to remain viable. Moreover, the level of fees
is directly related to the quantity and quality of services to be provided to a predetermined population group. There are well-known
problems associated with these constraints: benefit restrictions, income barriers to enrollment, escalation of premiums and competition
with like groups. These are precisely the problems NHCs were designed to obviate. In our view, the present general medical care
situation requires coexistence of NHCs and HMOs, not the transformation of the former into the latter.

CONCLUDING REMARKS

The first five chapters of the present monograph were aimed at identifying major facets of accountability in a variety of health facility settings. In this concluding chapter we have focused on certain weak strands in the accountability network identified earlier and have made suggestions for shoring up as well as enlarging the linkages, to the end that the network as a whole will become strengthened.

Two points should be emphasized here. The first is that the process of improving accountability mechanisms must be a continuing one in order to cope with the dynamics of change in the health care delivery system. The second is that the need for continuous study and review of means to enhance accountability transcends whatever changes in financing mechanisms may transpire in the near future. It should be obvious that a National Health Insurance scheme will require more attention to the questions of accountability, not less.

In this work our bias has been implicit (if not at various points explicit) that accountability mechanisms are more effective if they are built in and formal rather than ad hoc and informal. [37] The approach taken here coincides in part with the view expressed recently by Kerr L. White:[38]

> Many failures in the maintenance of quality are
> systems failures, not physician failures. The way
> to get at the root of these failures is to start with
> boards of trustees and directors, hospital admin-
> istrators, and health care managers and hold them
> accountable in relatively simple terms for the care
> provided in their institutions and systems, just as
> boards and managements of airlines are held account-
> able for many systems failures and even for aircraft
> crashes.

White's emphasis in this quotation is on the negative aspects of accountability and on the quality aspect alone, whereas in this essay the positive aspects were stressed and we have included as well the elements of cost, governance, and kind of care as integral parts of the accountability question.

Finally—and this is one aspect of the matter to which we have not paid sufficient attention—we should consider the role of the professional himself. Brian Abel-Smith, [39] an author with intimate knowledge of and experience with the quarter-century-old British National Health Service wrote in this regard:

> Ultimately, we must look not just at the financial
> incentives of those who operate our health services,
> but at their ethos, their commitment and what gives
> them satisfaction in their job. . . . We will not get
> value for money in health care until health profes-
> sionals see it is part of their responsibility to see
> that we do.

In concluding this overview, I wish to reiterate that our approach
to this question has been one of separating out what we consider to be
the major elements comprising the accountability question, of assessing the effectiveness of these elements, and of suggesting means for
strengthening the elements themselves and the linkages among them.
Of necessity, this approach stressed formal rather than informal
modes of accountability, though doubtless another book could be
written centering solely around the latter theme. What I hope has been
accomplished here minimally is that the patient has been opened,
that some corrective surgery has been performed, and that the problems exposed will attract hands more skilled than my own to continue
with the task.

NOTES

1. Ronald Kessler in Washington Post, October 29, 1972, p. 1.
Succeeding articles appeared on October 30, 31, and November 1, 2,
and 3, 1972.
2. "The Cost of Health Care in New York State, A Six Month
Interim Report, prepared by the Temporary State Commission on
Living Costs and the Economy," April 1974, pp. 35-40.
3. New York Times, July 10, 1974.
4. "Seminar on Medical Staff Law," American College of Hospital
Administrators, Health Law Center, Aspen Systems Corporation
(n.d.).
5. Amitai Etzioni, "Alternative Conceptions of Accountability,"
Part 2, Hospital Progress, July 1974, p. 57.
6. New York Times, June 27, 1974, p. 1.
7. Brian Abel-Smith, "Value for Money in Health Services,"
Social Security Bulletin 37, no. 7 (July 1974), pp. 17ff.
8. Amitai Etzioni, "PSRO: A Poor Mechanism and a Possible
Alternative," American Journal of Public Health 64, no. 5 (May
1974), p. 507.
9. Irving Leveson, "Financing and Regulation of Health Services,"
Office of Program Analysis, Planning and Budgeting, New York City
Health Services Administration, November 1973 (processes), pp. 22-28.

10. Abel-Smith, op. cit., p. 22.

11. Anne R. Somers, "State Regulation of Hospitals and Health Care: The New Jersey Story," Blue Cross Reports, Research Series No. 11, July 1973, p. 16. For detailed evaluation of hospital regulation in New Jersey see, Bureaucratic Malpractice, a report by the Center for Analysis of Public Issues, Princeton, N. J., 1974.

12. New York Times, April 2, 1974.

13. Harry I. Greenfield, Hospital Efficiency and Public Policy (New York: Praeger Publishers, 1973).

14. New York Times, October 4, 1974.

15. Ibid.

16. Heal Yourself, Report of the Citizens Board of Inquiry Into Health Services for Americans, 2nd. ed. (Washington, D. C.: American Public Health Association, 1972), p. 131.

17. S. David Pomrinse, "To What Degree are Hospitals Publicly Accountable?" Hospitals 43 (February 16, 1969), p. 43.

18. Report of the Task Force on Medicaid and Related Programs, Department of Health, Education, and Welfare, 1970, p. 72

19. Ibid., p. 73.

20. Edward V. Sparer, "On the Matter of Community Relations: The Consumer Movement in Health Care and the Albert Eistein Medical Center," presented at the Long Range Planning Seminar, June 17, 1971, p. 39.

21. Ibid., p. 9.

22. Final Report, Texas Consumer Participation in Health Planning Project of the American Friends Service Committee, Philadelphia, July 20, 1973, pp. 5-8ff.

23. Sheila Wellington and Gary L. Tischler, "Community Mental Health: Why the Benign Neglect?," Yale Review of Law and Social Action 3, no. 1 (Fall 1972), p. 83.

24. Peter B. Terenzio, "Responsibilities of the Urban Hospital to the Community," Hospital Progress, September 1969, p. 94.

25. "Advisory Statement on American Hospital Association's Role in Consumer Health Education," Annual Reports, American Hospital Association, 1973, p. 63.

26. Health Perspective published by the Consumer Commission on the Accreditation of Health Services, Inc., April 1973, vol. 1, no. 1, p. 1. See also Donald K. Ross, A Public Citizen's Action Manual (New York: Grossman Publishers, 1973), particularly chap. 2.

27. New York Times, October 27, 1973, p. 51.

28. New York Times, October 11, 1974, p. 43.

29. Ross, op. cit., pp. 103-104.

30. See for example "Principles and Policies for Insuring Citizen Rights and Increasing Citizen Participation in Mental Hygiene

Programs, " and "The Final Report of the Task Force on Greater Community Involvement and Citizen Participation in Department of Mental Hygiene Programs, " New York State Department of Mental Hygiene, Albany, May 20, 1973, passim.

31. New York Times, October 7—10, 1974.

32. Materials on Health Law, Vol. 4, The Nursing Home, prepared by the Health Law Project, University of Pennsylvania Law School. rev. ed. , 1972, pp. 124-132.

33. Ibid. , pp. 132-134.

34. Ibid. , pp. 116-119.

35. New York Times, November 8, 1974, p. 43.

36. "Medicaid in New York: Utopianism and Bare Knuckles in Public Health, " Symposium reprinted from American Journal of Public Health 59, no. 5 (May 1969).

37. Cf. Amitai Etzioni, "Alternative Conceptions of Account-ability, " Hospital Progress, June 1974, Part 1.

38. Kerr L. White, "Health and Health Care: Personal and Public Issues, " the 1974 Michael M. Davis Lecture, University of Chicago Center for Health Administration Studies, Graduate School of Business.

39. Abel-Smith, op. cit. , p. 27. The same point is emphasized also in Rudolf Klein and Phoebe Hall, "Caring for Quality in the Caring Services, " Centre for Studies in Social Policy, Doughty Street Paper No. 2 (1974), London.

EPILOGUE: ALTERNATIVE CONCEPTIONS OF ACCOUNTABILITY

Amitai Etzioni

We shall first discuss alternative conceptions of accountability in health administration, then the consequences of this analysis for the education of health administrators. The separation is doubly necessary as (1) we must have an understanding of the underlying forces before we can formulate a sound educational policy, and (2) an analysis such as the one which follows is in itself a major potential educational tool. It can serve in the important task of sensitizing health administrators to contrasting conceptions of accountability.

THE SYMBOLIC USES OF ACCOUNTABILITY

Speakers and writers calling for greater accountability typically employ the term to refer to greater responsibility and responsiveness in three concrete contexts: to the needs of patients; towards those of the "community" (generally a euphemism for blacks, Mexican-Americans, American Indians or other minorities, especially a large minority living in the vicinity of the hospital); or toward "values" (for example, as in the phrase "higher standards of morality"). The unifying thread is the symbolic use of accountability. Though it may

---

*I wish to thank Pamela Doty and Nancy Castleman who served as research assistants for this part of the report. A previous version of this was published in Hospital Progress 55, nos. 5 and 6 (June and July, 1974).

not necessarily be—indeed perhaps rarely is—the consciously intended meaning, the chief meaning which in fact emerges is that of accountability as gesture. The hallmark of accountability as gesture is that it is pure norm with little or no instrumentality attached. That is, the speaker or writer advocating accountability fails to follow up the use of the term by outlining specific arrangements—for example, that patients be made the controlling force on hospital boards or that minorities be allotted a third of the beds; if such suggestions are made at all, the virtue held out for them is fully matched by their vagueness. Making "more information" available to the public is such a suggestion as in the following quote from a statement of policy and program by the Community Health Institute of New York City: "Those who provide health services to the public must be accountable to that public. This then requires that the people have access to all the relevant information needed to make accountability real. Accountability to the public is essential for public control."[1] Thus the prime function of "accountability" here is that by using the word the speaker declares himself "on the side of the angels." Rather than outlining a mechanism he is articulating or reaffirming a value position.

The sociological significance of such expressions, gestures, utterances, however, is more varied than one might immediately think. The point can be readily illustrated by reflecting on the differential significance of the word "integration" as used in the early 1960s, in each case symbolically, by the following types of persons: a white legislator endorsing integration to his black constituents, but failing to introduce or support bills enforcing specific aspects of integration; a black civil rights leader such as Martin Luther King or Roy Wilkins building a social movement; a white minister exhorting his white congregation in Scarsdale against racism.

The first use is inauthentic and manipulatory. When divorced from any systematic efforts to promote actual attainment of the desired values, "accountability" becomes a thin cover for inaction, a "Sunday only" value mechanically acknowledged in a secular form of lip service. This kind of "accountability" can be easily and vociferously endorsed by boards of trustees, insurance lobbyists, and others in positions of power whose recitations of the phrase serve as a substitute for actual accountability. It becomes then only a verbal concession, like the rhetoric of the Kerner Commission Report, with little provision for follow-through, as a direct drain of the pressures to "do something" about the situation.

Murray Edelman in his book The Symbolic Uses of Politics devoted a good deal of space to a discussion of such hortatory uses of political slogans. According to Edelman, the solemn ritual incantation of political slogans by those in charge of formulating or carrying out policy unaccompanied by any affective attempts to achieve the goals

incanted is particularly likely to occur in a situation where a large
but politically unorganized group that feels itself threatened desires
certain resources or power whose fulfillment would entail the opposition of a small, politically organized group or groups with an
effective interest in the resources or the substantive power claimed.[2]
Under such circumstances it is tempting for the politicians or administrators to satisfy the desires of those in the first groups for symbolic
reassurance (that they are not being ignored or that their interests
will be protected). Often, symbolic reassurance from power wielders
will provoke quiescence in an unorganized group—at the very least
because it takes the edge off dissatisfaction and makes the difficulties
of mobilization greater.[3] This quiescence may be quite temporary,
soon yielding to a reawakening of demand and a resentment over being
manipulated. But those who merely mouth accountability do not concern themselves with the longer run. In this vein Wilbur Rich has
written in Administration in Mental Health[4] that, "Mental health
administrators . . . view mandates from politicians for accountability
as a political games posture that will relax itself after the budget
hearings. Administrators affect a defensive posture and tighten their
monitoring of operating facilities to discourage public incidents.
Curious legislators have to be "educated" and administrators need to
be told they are not running a private domain. The media report these
encounters as public officials overseeing the bureaucracy. This reaction has almost become an annual game in which each participant is
aware of the rules, and the public is led to believe something is being
done. After the usefulness of the game has been exhausted, everybody
agrees that a better job needs to be done and goes home (Edelman,
1967). However, the scarcity of public resources and the coming of
the 'true believer'—the researcher—have made the game more difficult to play."

In their attempts to mobilize followers political and social movement leaders also use slogans and cue words—perhaps even the same
word that is being used by the power wielders in an attempt to provide
symbolic reassurance. In this context, however, though the use is still
symbolic the meaning is quite different. While group leaders may
still be dealing largely with gestures rather than mechanisms, "accountability" in this instance serves as a rallying point around which mobilization can be affected and a movement built. In such a situation the
demand for "accountability" becomes a shared symbol of all those
individuals galvanized into a political force which aims at seeking and
gaining specific concessions.[5] Once there is such an organized force,
the question of how accountability can be actualized may be confronted
immediately, or it may only be a step away, or it may be deliberately
deferred as a bargaining technique.

Somewhere in between the "coopting" and inauthentic use of slogans as a political tranquilizer unresponsive to basic needs and its issue flagging, group rallying use by leaders seeking to mobilize a constituency is the use of "accountability" as the banner of a campaign for moral education. Typically such a campaign is undertaken by one professional vis-a-vis his fellows or by a concerned but unselfinterested outsider. The moral educator views those he proselytizes in a manner very much akin to the way a socially conscious minister views his congregation: as persons basically anxious to do right by their values and their fellow-men, but whose behavior is not what it should be either because of lack of knowledge or improper education, or because they have not been reminded of their duties, or because insufficiently "good" models suitable for emulation have been set before them. Thus exhortation, moral suasion, lay preaching, and example setting are relied upon instead of introducing new accountability mechanisms—not to be inauthentic, but because these approaches are sincerely believed to be effective.

Dr. Avedis Donabidian attributes the tendency in health administration to emphasize moral education over regulations to the norm of colleaguing among physicians and the weakness of the formal and informal control that administrators have vis-a-vis physicians. He writes,

> The administrator must . . . determine the proper
> balance between the educational objectives of quality
> assessment and the need to deter and detect careless
> or incompetent practice. . . .
> In real life, the answer appears to depend in part
> on the role and influence of the practicing physicians
> on the program. Wherever this influence is small,
> as in some health insurance programs, there is
> either no responsibility for quality or, at best,
> emphasis is placed on the identification and correc-
> tion of abuse that borders on the criminal. Where-
> ever the role of the practicing physician is significantly
> large or dominant, the emphasis may fall so predom-
> inantly on the educational objective that the disciplin-
> ary objective is in danger of being ignored or explicitly
> excluded. Many factors account for this imbalance.
> Fundamentally, the control of behavior within the
> medical profession is brought about not by the co-
> ercive power of superior authority, but by the op-
> eration of ethical standards that prescribe respon-
> sibility to patients and sensitivity to the good opinion
> of colleagues. This fundamental orientation is re-
> inforced by notions concerning the nature and frequency

of deviations from accepted practice and what
accounts for them. It is asserted that most
physicians are motivated to provide good care
and to use the hospital in an appropriate manner.
Deviations are believed to be caused by occasional
inattention, by gradual, unintentional drift into bad
habits or technical obsolescence, or by pervasive
administrative and organizational constraints over
which the physician has little control. Flagrant
abuse is said to be a rare phenomenon. As a consequence, significant improvements in the levels
of care, and savings in hospital days inappropriately
used, are not likely to be achieved by detecting and
correcting abuse, but by bringing about smaller,
and more pervasive changes in the practice of a
much larger number of physicians. It is the cumula-
tive effect of these smaller adjustments, influencing
the mass of physicians, that is expected to pay the
greatest dividends. Finally, any approach that leads
to the exclusion or elimination of specified physicians
from program participation is considered to be socially
undesirable because it simply permits the physician to
continue practice in the general community, unsupported
and unsupervised. [6]

As different as these uses of "accountability" are, however, they
all rely upon it as a symbol rather than as a social force and, unfortunately, tend to run into one another. As a result, when a health
administrator talks up accountability one often has a difficult time
discerning whether his gestures are inauthentic, rallying, or ed-
ucationalistic. Their social consequences will depend to a considerable
extent on the other accountability processes, which we explore next.

ACCOUNTABILITY AS REALPOLITIK

A contrasting view of accountability is that of an existing pattern
of administration and government that reflects at any particular point
in time the sum total of the forces working on the system, those working
to maintain the status quo, and those seeking to reshape it. Such an
outlook adapts to health administration the interest group theories of
politics espoused by such political analysts as Robert Dahl, David
Truman, V. O. Key, and Earl Latham. [7] From this perspective the
hospital is viewed as a polity, affected by its members and by outside

forces, in the continual act of restructuring. Apart from its bookkeeping and managerial functions in the narrow sense, hospital administration is a political process through which various groupings negotiate, confront, or adjust their claims. Thus "accountability" becomes the actual degree to which the hospital administration is responsive to the claims and demands of the particular interests of doctors, nurses, union, or activist patients. The hospital administrator is seen as being located at the center of this process—the focal point of the pressures—not at the top, in charge. The hospital administrator's position in this theory in fact is analagous to that of a billiard ball in a physics diagram upon which various forces impinge. Typically, the hospital administrators' actions are seen as almost totally determined by various partisan interest group pressures; predicting his reactions then is a matter of knowing the coefficients of strength of the various groups.

Even when the hospital administrator is known to have views of his own and a modicum of autonomy, he is not seen as representing the interests of the polity as a whole but as having his own "vested interests," that are similarly parochial to those of the pressure groups influencing him. In general, the interests imputed to him are those of the bureaucrat seeking either to expand his domain or, most especially, to defend his own incumbency in authority.[8] Such a view of hospital administration and "accountability" we label "Realpolitik" because in it power is viewed as the only significant variable.

The rules of Realpolitik are fairly well known. To list them here briefly is of course to report, not bless, their existence. By and large, groups with more status, income, education, have more power and hence make the system relatively more "accountable" to them. They have more leverage. Accordingly one would expect a typical American voluntary hospital (and its administration and administrator) to be most "accountable" to the physicians and/or trustees; less so to the nurses and aides; least so to the patients; especially inattentive to the poor, uneducated, nonpaying customers. In terms of the typical American community, one would expect it to be most responsive to the local business community, and less so to other groups. As a rule, more responsive to government agencies of various levels; less to "consumers" groups and advocates.

Different types of hospitals—municipal, proprietary, or voluntary—are expected to vary in the groups they respond to most readily and in wealth, status, "pull" in government, potential voting strength, or other kinds of power bases, which has the greatest leverage. For instance, we might expect voluntary hospitals to be rather more insulated from the pressures of city politics than the municipal hospitals but rather more dependent upon the good will and continued munificence of the cities' "first families."[9]

Some evidence that different interest groups possess differential
amounts of power in different types of hospitals is given by an analysis
of data collected by the Michigan Health and Social Security Institute
on the membership of the boards of trustees of 48 Detroit area hospitals. They found that in the category of nonosteopathic, nongovernmental, nonreligiously run not-for-profit hospitals, more than 50 percent of the board members were executives and lawyers. By contrast,
on local government run hospital boards, executives and lawyers
numbered no more than 11 percent of the board members. On the
local hospital boards in general, there was less business representation and greater community diversification, including public officials,
educators, union officials, foremen, a consumer consultant, a safety
consultant, a housewife, a farmer and an industrial relations consultant. [10]

In addition, groups will differ in their leverage, over time,
depending to the extent they are organized and mobilized to affect the
particular polity. Thus if the physicians act chiefly as individuals
they will obtain fewer resources than if they set up hospital-wide
committees, aiming to insure that their collective preferences will
carry. And, as a rule, unionized hospital workers will be more
"accounted to" than unorganized ones. Even patients, represented by
patients' advocates, ombudsmen, lawyers, or consumer representatives—being weak and easy to deflect—will, according to this view,
gain in more ways than they would without any of these organizations
and mobilizing devices.

Empirical support for the view that the nature of power constel-
lations in hospitals changes over time is given by Charles Perrow in
an historical case study tracing changes in goals and power in a
voluntary general hospital from 1885 to 1958. The period 1885 to
1929 was found to be one of trustee domination, reflecting the overriding importance of obtaining capital and community legitimation.
The much lesser power of the doctors testified to the still primitive
state of medical science at the time. The hospital was organized as
a charity hospital under Jewish auspices and its prime function was
to provide free care to impoverished Jews and other needy persons.
From 1929 to 1942 the balance of power shifted to the doctors, a
change directly related to the enormous technical advances made in
medical science beginning in the first 30 years of the century and
continuing on. The emphasis on free care declined greatly, and in
line with the priorities of the doctors, service was oriented toward
paying patients. And the hospital began to seek prestige in terms that
the medical profession recognized: through research. From 1942 to
1952 an "administrative challenge" arose to correct some of the abuse
that had arisen due to medical domination. Because the administrator
was a doctor he could achieve hegemony in the medical area as well as

the strictly administrative aspects of the hospital. The period of
multiple leadership (1952-1958) began when a new administrator was
hired and a clear demarcation made between the expressive and in-
strumental elites, giving each increased autonomy in its own area.
Meanwhile a conflict between the previous administrator and the
medical staff had led the former to seek allies among the hitherto
dormant trustees. A temporary coalition was formed between the
administrator and the reactivated trustees but eventually the board
evolved into an independent third force. By 1958 then the leadership
included three roughly equal parties: the administration, the trustees,
and the doctors. Multiple leadership according to Perrow leads to
three types of decision making—the fortuitous convergence of interests,
segregated decision making, and the piecemeal accumulation of small
victories. Though the dominance of one group is avoided, the balance
of power places a premium on harmony and avoidance of conflict with
the drawback that long-range planning tends to be neglected, since it
could expose conflicting interests. [11]

This "hard-headed" view suggest that the phrase "more accountable" is meaningless; the question is: more accountable to whom?
The implication is that accountability to one group means almost by
definition, less accountability to another. Implicit in the Realpolitik
position is that values per se—as represented by the moral education
of the administrator—count for almost nothing. A change in the
relative power of the various groups is the only factor that could be
expected to produce a significant change in accountability.

THE FORMAL, LEGAL APPROACH

Many in the health field subscribe to a view of accountability that
defines it in legal or formal terms. The emphasis is on instituting
"checks and balances." In the academic world, such a concentration
was once current in political science, though it has waned over the
past 20 years, and is still quite popular in the field of public administration. Game theory and cybernetics are more or less in this
vein of thinking also.

In hospital administration this approach sees the administrator
as having to be made "accountable" to one or more authorities (the
board, his superior, the law), and much ink is shed to clarify these
legalities. A case point is the question: if a doctor misbehaves in a
hospital, who is legally accountable—the doctor alone, the hospital
and its administrator alone, or both?

In a recent California malpractice case (Albert Gonzales v. John
G. Nork M.D. and Mercy General Hospital of Sacramento) the judge
found both the hospital and the doctor responsible for the patient's

damages. He awarded Gonzales $1.7 million in compensatory damages against both defendants and $2 million in punitive damages against the physician alone. The hospital attorneys argued that since the medical staff of the hospital was self-governing with regard to professional work, the hospital could not be held responsible for Nork's performance of needless surgery on Gonzales and a series of others, most of whom suffered neurologic deficits as a result. The judge disagreed, stating "The hospital, by virtue of its custody of the patient, owes him a duty of care; this duty includes the obligation to protect him from acts of malpractice by his independently retained physician who is a member of the hospital staff if the hospital knows or has reason to know or should have know that such acts were likely to occur." He then ruled that the repeated bad surgical results obtained by Dr. Nork should have been recognized by Mercy's staff peer review committees, set up pursuant to the hospital's bylaws, and that Dr. Nork's surgical practice should have been restricted.[12] Similar rulings were handed down in a number of other recent cases: a 1965 Illinois Supreme Court decision, Darling v. Charleston Community Memorial Hospital, a 1972 Nevada Supreme Court decision, George L. Moore v. Board of Carson Tahoe Hospital, and a 1972 Arizona Appellate decision, Kay L. Purcell v. Zimbleman.[13]

Along related lines, there have been attempts to make hospitals more accountable to the public-at-large by requiring them to file detailed financial statements, and various mechanisms have been proposed to make such financial statements easily accessible to interested parties.

In addition, laws have been put through requiring the participation of consumers on Hill-Burton advisory councils and on state and regional Comprehensive Health Planning organizations.[14]

Recent changes in hospital accreditation procedures are permitting consumers and consumer organizations to participate in the accreditation process by learning when the biannual accreditations surveys of hospitals in their areas are to be held and being present at an information interview to state complaints as they relate to the standards of the Joint Commission of Accreditation of Hospitals.[15]

In an effort to make doctors and hospitals more accountable to the government in spending of Medicare and Medicaid monies, Congress recently enacted the PSRO legislation designed to subject old and poor patients' admission to a hospital to preadmission review in all but emergency cases by local committees of doctors.

A tougher proposal requiring an in-hospital committee review of Medicare admissions to crack down on needless hospitalization or protracted stays was dropped by the Social Security Administration after drawing heavy fire from the AMA.[16]

Structural changes within the hospital are similar measures, because they work on the basis of changes in formal definitions. Thus,

requiring that hospitals have a consumer representative on the board
is a case in point; it is said to make the hospital more accessible.

Along these lines OEO guidelines dictated that OEO and Public
Health Service-funded neighborhood health centers had to form either
governing boards or advisory committees composed of at least one-
third "democratically selected representatives of the poor."[17]

Similarly, there have been experiments in some health units with
patients' advocates, patients' rights organizations, and formalized
grievance procedures. For example, at Yale-New Haven Hospital a
patient's advocate program was set up by the Dixwell Legal Rights
organization. The woman hired to be the patients' advocate was a resident of the community, had 13 years experience as a practical nurse,
and was given 10 months paralegal training by the Dixwell Organization.
At Coler Hospital in New York, a chronic disease facility, three
different patients organizations whose stances range from conservative
to radical have managed through union-style action to substantially
increase the civil rights of the chronic care patients housed in the
institution. Among the gains achieved: the city has been forced to
register over 350 voters on Welfare Island, many of whom have been
residents of the hospital for more than ten years; voting machines
have been promised for election day, and the hospital's right to open
mail before giving it to patients—particularly Social Security checks,
which the hospital then distributed along with signover slips—has been
challenged in court. The Martin Luther King Jr. Center in the Bronx,
has set up a patient's rights program which includes a definition of
patients' rights program which includes a definition of patients' rights,
mechanisms for dissemination of these rights to the community, and
the establishment of a systematic procedure for their enforcement.
All registrants at the Center are to receive a patients' rights manual,
a grievance form, and information about the grievance procedure.
The rights covered include privacy, confidentiality, and consent,
all explained in concrete terms readily understandable to the registrants.[18]

Many social scientists are skeptical of such formal and legal
accountability mechanisms. According to the most popular introductory
textbook in sociology (Sociology, by Leonard Broom and Philip
Selznick),

> The rules of the formal system account for much but
> but by no means all of the patterned behavior in associa-
> tions. The phrase "informal structure" is used to denote
> those patterns that emerge from the spontaneous inter-
> action of personalities and groups within the organization.
> . . . An organization's informal structure is made up of

the patterns that develop when the participants face
persistent problems that are not provided for by the
formal system. These problems arise in a variety
of ways:

    1. Impersonality of the formal system. The definite
rules and prescribed roles of the formal structure are
necessarily impersonal. . . . In practice, it is often
necessary to reach individuals as persons, if their best
efforts and their highest loyalty are to be mustered. . . .

    2. Lag of the formal system. . . . The formal system
of an organization tends to lag behind changes in its operations. . . . Despite the lag, those who do the work must
solve new problems, even if these problems have not
yet been recognized officially and there are no rules to
meet them. . . . The temporary solution may be an
informal consultation. . . .

    3. Generality of the formal system. The rules that
make up the formal system are general. . . . In every
organization there are some informal patters that provide more detailed control than the formal system. In
time some of these patterns may become formalized;
others will remain outside official recognition. . . .
By keeping rules general, ways of acting may be
tested informally before they are given official approval. . . .

    4. Personal problems and interests. . . . Informal
structure arises as the individual brings into play problems and interests other than those defined by his role
in the organization.[19]

The consumer representative often turns out to be not "the
peoples'" representative, but a businessman rather similar to the
other board members in background and outlook. Or such positions
may be monopolized by various types of "health professionals" who
may not always agree with the doctors, but who are not average
consumers either. In addition, consumers on hospital boards often
learn that formal entitlements do not necessarily confer real power,
as stockholders long ago discovered in business corporations. The
power wielders may hold their own meeting in a back room prior to
the formal meeting, which then becomes a mere ceremony. Or the
doctors and administrators may have their way via the phenomenon
of "partisan analysis"—if the consumers have no independent source
of information they may have no way of arriving at and documenting
a point of view opposing the administrative one. Similarly, the aura
of expertise surrounding doctors and administrators versus the low

social status of the consumer representatives can be expected to contribute to the likelihood that the consumer representatives will defer to the hospital officials. In addition, while the doctors and administrators have a continuing personal vested interest in the affairs of the hospital, the motivations of consumer representatives are more likely to be altruistic. Unless the position of consumer representative is one which confers great prestige in the persons' social circle, or unless there is some other reward, there seems little incentive to attend meetings often and regularly and to engage in the necessary self-education. It seems almost inevitable for enthusiasm to decline over time.

There are analagous problems with relying on consumer grievance procedures to insure "accountability." The chief drawback is that consumers are usually quite unable to judge for themselves the technical aspects of the medical care they receive. The truth of this observation is strikingly highlighted by the results of a study in which judgments of expert assessors were compared with the opinions of those who received the care in question. "For cases in which care was judged to have been excellent or good, 86 percent of patients expressed the opinion that they had received the "best" care. For cases judged by experts to have been fair or poor, 74 percent of patients felt they had received the best care. At the same time, in the second category of cases only five percent of patients said the care received had been "not good."[20]

Yet while the social science caveat that not all that glitters with accountability truly enhances it seems to be revalidated here, nevertheless, on balance, formal mechanisms do have an effect—especially when coupled with efforts to build consensus around values and to mobilize power through coalition building as discussed below. Thus a study of the accomplishments of thirty-seven Massachusetts Mental Health and Retardation Area Boards on which citizen participation had been required by legislation revealed four separate types of board accomplishment, each one resulting from a different strategy pursued by the board: service creation or improvement, mobilization of outside resources (from state and federal government), achievement of local autonomy (mobilization of resources from the private sector or the local government), and coordination (integration of the efforts of a variety of social agencies).[21]

Although consumer representation on decision making and advisory bodies overseeing health units has received the most attention as the solution to the problems of instituting accountability to the public at large, it is by no means the only mechanism available. Another promising approach is that of the regularly scheduled Comprehensive Health Audit (CHA). The principle behind the notion of the CHA is essentially the same as that behind the annual financial audit in the corporate world. In the case of the corporate financial audit, the law requires than an outside expert licensed by the government (a CPA) review the books of the joint stock company on a yearly basis so as to insure "accountability" of the firm and its managers to the stockholders or legal owners of the corporation. The CHA would entail a regular assessment of cost-consciousness and quality of care delivered in each hospital by an outside team of health auditors licensed by the government. The chief advantages of the CHA are that (1) it accords well with the American philosophy of harnessing the profit motive in the service of the public interest, (2) it avoids the necessity of setting up a costly and cumbersome governmental regulatory apparatus (which as we know from historical experience has typically ended by serving the purposes of those it was intended to watchdog), and (3) it relies upon a tried-and-true mechanism known to be efficient in one area and tranfers it to a closely related field. The chief disadvantage of the CHA is that "input" measurements are so much more refined than "output" measures. Until more accurate output indices are developed CHAs will have to employ fairly crude measures and their evaluations will not be nearly so reliable as the financial audit. [22]

A "GUIDANCE" APPROACH

The following view of accountability—the "guidance" approach—is, I should hasten to admit, the view closest to my heart. It took me six hundred-odd pages to spell it out elsewhere. [23] Let me simply suggest here its chief points relevant to the issue at hand.

As I see it, accountability is based on a variety of interacting forces, not one lone attribute or mechanism. The direction the administrator takes, in accountability as in other matters, is affected by all the factors already listed and some others still to be mentioned. In part, he responds to articulations of "rights" on the part of "the community," its leaders, the press, and so on—that is, to claims of accountability. In part, his accountability is circumscribed and delineated by the legalities and formalities of the state and the like. Hence changes in any and all of these factors are effective ways to change the level and scope of accountability; none of them is all-inclusive.

Moreover, several missing elements must still be added to complete the analysis. For example, in contrast to those who see power as the core explanatory factor, I see accountability as having both a power and a moral base, in the sense that the values which administrators "internalize" (as well as those of other participants, both in the health unit under consideration and persons acting on it from the outside), do both affect the direction the health unit takes. Thus, in a recent study by the Center for Policy Research, Steven Beaver and Rosita Albert found (in a study of which I am the principal investigator, supported by NIMH) that the administrators of several hospitals studied were more progressive on several acounts, than either the people in the area served by the hospital, or their patient-advocate, activist leaders. For example, neighborhood residents, community leaders, and hospital administrators in a major United States city were asked: "which of these three kinds of health care do you think is the most important for this community? (a) routine problems (checkups, maternal and child care, dental and eye care, ordinary sicknesses), (b) care of major body illnesses (heart problems, cancer, operations), (c) care for socially relevant problems (drug addiction, mental illness, alcoholism)." While a full 80 percent of the hospital administrators chose the "socially relevant problems" as the most important kind of health care problem for the neighborhood, smaller proportions of the neighborhood residents and community leaders chose this alternative—60 percent and 52 percent respectively. Routine problems were judged as most important by 31 percent of the community residents, 35 percent of the leaders, and 20 percent of the hospital administrators. Major body illnesses were seen as the most important health care problem to 9 percent of the neighborhood dwellers, 14 percent of their leaders, and to none of the administrators. Thus while majorities of all three groups believe that problems such as drug addiction, mental illness, and alcoholism are the major health problems of the community under study, a clearly higher percentage of the hospital administrators holds to this view. While the differences are not sizable, it is nevertheless significant that they remained consistent across a broad spectrum of questions answered by the three groups.

This study merely illustrates what we all know from personal experience: that administrators are not neutral beings. They have sentiments, preferences, and above all, values—although, of course, the differ greatly among themselves as to what they value, how clearly they perceive their values, and how far they are willing to go in promoting their values against those of others (say those of M. D. s) if a difference should become evident. The content and intensity of these value commitments are in part affected by the administrator's education, a point to which we shall return.

The administrator need not be merely a broker of power, a meeting point of various internal and external pressures which he adapts the way a vectorgram would; adapting to the strongest pressure at the moment, although it often comes rather close to that. Aside from his personal values and position of authority in the structure (which give him a separate backbone—that is, a measure of direction other than the Realpolitik of give and take) there is, in addition, an opportunity for creative leadership.

I do not see the capacity for leadership as consisting of abstract, moralistic character traits; I see these as specific skills. The object is not to fly in the face of reality or power groups, nor to wildly pursue utopian notions of social justice or accountability (such an administrator is all too likely to be quickly expelled) but to help shape, mobilize, and combine the vectors which determine the health unit's direction and accountability model so as to bring them closer to the desired system. To shape these forces requires educating the various groups to definitions and demands which are closer to what is legal and ethical and just. This is probably the most difficult part of the creative administrator's job.

Also, for the administrator to mobilize one or more of the relevant groups is to bring about a change in the balance of vectors to which the administrator must later respond. Thus if the physicians are putting undue pressure on him to take a course of action he considers undesirable, he may instigate a greater activization of the board or of consumer representatives to serve as countervailing forces, somewhat changing the vectorgram. This course often cannot be followed because it leads to a measure of countermobilization by the other group—in this case the M.D. s—realizing next to no net change but creating a higher level of conflict all around. [24]

Somewhat better opportunities for creative leadership are open to the administrator in the area of coalition forming. Coalitions arise, not necessarily explicitly, when two or more groups favor the same or a similar course of action. They may be composed of insiders only, or varying combinations. For example, Lowell Bellin when First Deputy Commissioner of the New York Department of Public Health succeeded in forming a coalition between his agency and the consumers to push a number of voluntary hospitals into giving more resources and attention to ambulatory care. [25] The context was the New York State Ghetto Medicine program which institutionalized the coalition between the Public Health Department and consumers by requiring each hospital desirous of obtaining funds under the program's provisions to (a) subject its ambulatory care services to contractual standard setting, monitoring, and enforcement by the New York City Department of Health, and (b) to become associated with an Ambulatory Services Advisory Committee, comprising a majority of consumer members. Twenty-two voluntary hospitals in New York City participated in the program. As Bellin et al. note in their American Journal of Public Health article, hospital-based ambulatory care services have always been low in the hierarchy of priorities of hospital administrations in comparison to their inpatient services. Thus the primary incentive for these hospitals to allow their ambulatory

care services to be scrutinized by the health department and a consumer group, in marked opposition to their autonomous institutional
traditions, was desperation for funds. Yet Bellin et al. point out also
that the simple mechanism of a contract between the hospitals and
the agency would never have sufficed to insure that the monies ear-
marked for ambulatory care actually were spent in that manner.

How to prevent the regulated agencies from regulating the reg-
ulators is a notorious problem in public administration, and by itself
the agency would never have had the resources to keep the hospitals
from reallocating the funds according to their own internal priorities.
Though originally skeptical about the value of working with relatively
uninformed and inexperienced consumers of hospital ambulatory
services, the Department concluded, however, that its alliance with
the consumers was vital in giving it the leverage which resulted in
widespread obedience of contractual stipulations by the hospitals. In
addition, quite a number of spin-off improvements in ambulatory care
which were not part of the original stipulations were obtained via
pressure put on the hospitals by the advisory committees, the Department, or the two in concert. In speaking about the accomplishments
of the Ghetto Medicine Program, Bellin listed the number of advances
that have emerged from this program of active collaboration between
consumers and professionals in private voluntary hospitals as follows:

1. Instituting a unit record system
2. Hiring an interpreter
3. Establishing a primary physician system
4. Developing a list of services for distribution
5. Hiring a full-time director of ambulatory care
6. Holding two open public hearings
7. Adding preventive medicine services
8. Assigning additional physicians, nurses, and clerks to the
   outpatient department
9. Eliminating underutilized clinics
10. Starting a community outreach program
11. Starting a new clinic or other services
12. Remodeling clinic and/or emergency room areas
13. Running patient-attitude surveys
14. Providing music and snack machines
15. Establishing a communication link between the medical board,
    administrators, and the consumers
16. Changing the referral system
17. Changing X-ray and laboratory follow-up
18. Extending clinical hours[26]

The reason coalition building is often effective is that while in isolation each vector is relatively given and unchangeable, the ways in which they may be combined to neutralize, to partially reinforce, or to fully back up one another is less fixed. The ultimate success lies in building a coalition in favor of greater accountability which is either very wide—or all-inclusive. Then the desired changes are introduced almost as if by themselves.

Closely related but even more productive is the formulation of new alternatives. Groups rarely have fully developed positions and almost always can find alternative ways toward their goals. [27] If ways can be found to allow them to advance their goals which at the same time lessen their opposition to other groups and to higher levels of accountability, then the program's success will be particularly pronounced. For example, the strength of the HMO pattern is said to be that it is both responsive to the doctors' legitimate needs and more responsive to the patients than solo practice; if this is the case, it is such a creative alternative. [28]

To advance any and all these strategies, the administrator needs a considerable understanding of how social systems work, how polities function, what the various groups' values and needs are, and what alternatives are practical and acceptable. In part he can get the needed knowledge from proper training; in part from continual interaction with the various groups inside and outside his unit, which impinge on it. Experience suggests that without fixed "institutionalized" opportunities for communication, such regularized interaction is unlikely to occur with sufficient frequency. The explanation of the mechanisms of institutional communication cannot be undertaken here, but they constitute a vital element of any effective accountability system. [29]

FROM UNIT TO SYSTEM,
AND THE NEW DEFINITION OF HEALTH

So far we have deliberately followed the prevailing tradition, dealing with the health unit (hospital, clinic, nursing home) as if it were a world unto itself. While the administrator has repeatedly been referred to as dealing with both internal and external forces, those were viewed as impinging on a unit of considerable integrity and cohesiveness. While this view is both necessary (we cannot take in the whole world; we must "break it up" into units to think about and to deal with it) and favored (especially in nongovernmental health units), health units are increasingly becoming part of large systems. (We do

not mean neat, well-consolidated systems, but simply more encompassing entities.)[30] The concern with accountability is, to a significant
extent, a concern with these larger entities.

In part, this is the case because accountability is significantly
affected by supervisory, regulatory, "higher order" structures,
especially government agencies and professional bodies. In part,
this is the case because administrators must manage health systems,
not just health units, and the manner in which these are managed
greatly affects the performance of the individual units. Last, but
equally important, greater accountability in one service area—such
as here in health—often requires corrections of ills in other sectors
of the society (sanitation, pollution control, highway safety, education)—that can only be activated via higher level units or inter
unit give and take. As an article by Blumstein and Zubkoff on governmental health policy puts it, "The concept of health has a large social
component. Illness may to a large degree be conditioned by culture,
and its definition may be the product of a social bargaining process."[31]
Later on they note that

> . . . health maintenance has begun to receive attention among
> health professionals, but the concept still carries with it a top-
> heavy medical service orientation. Most significant for our
> society, there are a considerable number of environmental
> factors which contribute substantially to our health problems;
> any governmental decision to become involved in the health
> sector must consider possible allocation alternatives in
> personal and nonpersonal areas as a means of promoting
> health.[32]

These environmental factors affecting health are divided into three
categories: (1) technological factors resulting from industrialization,
such as air pollution and unsafe working conditions, (2) personal
health maintenance factors such as life styles encouraging overeating
and underexercising, and (3) socioeconomic status, especially such
health related conditions associated with poverty as inadequate sanitation, overcrowded housing, and bad nutrition.[33]

EDUCATIONAL IMPLICATIONS

1. Education programs that train health administrators but
fail to provide them with a set of values to guide their behavior, serve
to encourage lack of accountability. Every program should make it
one of its cardinal commitments to develop the normative backbone

of the health administrators it trains. To increase the sensitivity of doctors and other health professionals to these matters, Senators Javits, Williams, and Mondale have recently submitted bill S-954 which amends the Public Health Service Act to provide "in the training of health professionals, for an increasing emphasis on the ethical, social, legal and moral implications of advances in biomedical research and technology."

This can be achieved only in part via the lecture course. Ethical education may perhaps be best advanced by presenting suitable cases for guided group discussion and through interaction with persons themselves committed to high normative standards. Hence the faculty entrusted with the education of health administrators needs to include persons of status in this realm, such as clergy who have dealt with dying patients, a hospital ombudsman, a community leader of high standards.

2. The educational program should sensitize future health administrators to the different conceptions of accountability as outlined above. The trainees should come to understand in a deep sense the benefits and drawbacks of passive (or neutral) versus active (or creative) administration; the limits of morality not backed by social forces; the role of formal factors; the significance, dangers, and limitations of mobilization versus coalition building, and so on. In effect, in our judgment, the whole preceding analysis is to be viewed as a course outline in accountability, to be backed up by more extended preparation in appropriate portions of social and political science curricula.

I say "appropriate" because these sciences contain segments that are as limited in their perspective as some of the monofactorial schools of accountability discussed above. For instance, some stress the role of free will and values per se; others are mesmerized by formal functions, and still others by Realpolitik. True, the more a student is exposed and sensitized to even these partial analyses of administration as a social and political system—instead of merely to accounting, financial management, and operations analysis—the more he will understand the processes of accountability and his own range of maneuverability. He may then piece together his own synthesis, maybe with the help of the above outline. Better still, of course, would be a program built around a social-political science approach which is encompassing and includes the necessary material.

Here again, lectures will do at best only part of the work. Case studies, in conjunction with guided group discussions, backed up with dialogue with experienced administrators would be more helpful. Later in the student's career a regular (say, weekly) workshop for administrators-in-training, during their "internship" period, might be most effective, because here the participant's own experience can be studied and incorporated as educational experience.

None of these ideas are novel, either as general educational procedure or as efforts in the training of health administrators. Novelty
would lie in new systematic combinations, along the suggested lines,
for the suggested purposes.

3. The preceding discussion has taken as its cornerstone an implicit assumption that should be explicated, both for the purposes of
this presentation and for the purposes of the educational effort we hope
will be built around accountability: that the administrator is at the
center of the guidance health units and systems and has a leading
responsibility for their direction. While special interests are real,
the administrator need not be merely the spokesman of interest groups
or a pawn of social forces. Neither is he only on the second string of
accountability while doctors man the first line; this is neither reliable
nor just. The administrator should have the ultimate responsibility.
At the same time, he would be woefully mistaken to see himself as
all powerful; an accountable system can arise only through broad
support, where the administrator may mobilize and educate but
cannot dictate.

NOTES

1. The Community Health Institute, Health Action Forum No.
1, November 1973.
2. Murray Edelman, The Symbolic Uses of Politics (Urbana:
University of Illinois Press, 1964), chap. 2.
3. Ibid.
4. Wilbur Rich, "Accountability Indices: The Search for the
Philosopher's Touchstone in Mental Health," Administration in Mental
Health, Fall 1973, pp. 7-8.
5. For a concrete example of "accountability" as a rallying slogan
in an attempt to build a social movement see Ralph Nader, ed., The
Consumer and Corporate Accountability. New York: Harcourt Brace
Jovanovich, Inc., 1973.
6. Avedis Donabidian, A Guide to Medical Care Administration,
Volume II: Medical Care Appraisal (New York: American Public
Health Association, 1969), pp. 100-101.
7. Hans J. Morgenthau's work is another example of this approach.
See Morgenthau, Politics Among Nations (New York: Alfred A. Knopf,
1954), and his Scientific Man vs. Power Politics (Chicago: University
of Chicago Press, Phoenix ed., 1965).
8. See, for example, Ray Elling, "The Hospital Support Game
in Urban Centers," in Eliot Freidson, ed., The Hospital in Modern
Society (New York: Free Press, 1963), pp. 73-111.

9. See Duncan Neuhauser and Fernand Turiotte, "Costs and
Quality of Care in Different Types of hospitals," The Annals of the
American Academy of Political and Social Science, The Nation's
Health: Some Issues, January 1972, pp. 50-61.

10. Private communication.

11. Charles Perrow, "Goals and Power Structures," in Eliot
Freidson, ed., The Hospital in Modern Society (New York: Free
Press, 1963), pp. 112-145.

12. David S. Rubsamen, "Doctor and the Law: How Responsible
is a Hospital for One of Its Surgeons?" Medical World News, February
15, 1974, p. 47.

13. Ibid.

14. For more information on this see the chapter entitled "Consumer Influence on the Federal Role" in Health Yourself, Report of the
Citizens Board of Inquiry Into Health Services for Americans.

15. Gerald Gold, "The Public Gets Voice in Accreditation of
Hospitals," New York Times, December 20, 1973.

16. "HEW Drops Tough Peer Review Plan," Medical World News,
October 5, 1973, p. 50.

17. For more on this, see "The Health Rights Defenders: All
Power to the Patients," Health-Pac Bulletin, October 1969.

18. Ibid., pp. 2-5.

19. Leonard Broom and Phillip Selznick, Sociology, 3rd. ed.
(New York: Harper & Row, 1963), pp. 227-229.

20. J. Erhlich, M. A. Morehead, and R. E. Trussell, The
Quantity, Quality and Costs of Medical and Hospital Care Secured by
a Sample of Teamster Families in the New York Area (New York:
Columbia University School of Public Health and Administrative
Medicine, 1962), quoted in A Guide to Medical Care Administration,
Vol. II: Medical Care Appraisal (New York: American Public Health
Association, 1969), p. 110. For examples and evaluations of more
and less successful consumer participation schemes see Jeoffrey B.
Gordon, "The Politics of Community Medicine Projects: A Conflict
Analysis" Medical Care 7, no. 6 (November-December 1969), pp.
419-428; Roger G. Larson, "Reactions to Social Pressure," Annual
Administrative Reviews 46 (April 1, 1972), pp. 181-186; Donna
Manderson and Markay Kerr, "Citizen Influence in Health Services
Programs," American Journal of Public Health 61, no. 8, pp. 1518-
1523; Frank M. Shepard and Beulah Wiley, "A Community-University
Cooperative Venture, Hospitals, JAHA 46 (September 16, 1972)
pp. 64-70; Wilfred E. Holton, Peter K. New, and Richard M. Messler,
"Citizen Participation and Conflict," Administration in Mental Health,
Fall 1973, pp. 96-103.

21. William R. Meyers, Jane Grisell, Albert Gollen, Patricia Papernow, Bellenden R. Hutcheson, and Erica Terlin, "Methods of Measuring Citizen Board Accomplishment in Mental Health and Retardation" Community Mental Health Journal 8, no. 4 (1972).

22. For an example of a prototype CHA, see Carol Brierly, "Hospital Costs: What the Figures Really Say," Prism, February 1974, pp. 12-17, 62-64.

23. Amitai Etzioni, The Active Society (New York: Free Press, 1968).

24. Etzioni, The Active Society, chaps. 15 and 18.

25. Lowell Elliezer Bellin, Florence Kavaler, and Al Schwartz, "Phase One of Consumer Participation in Policies of 22 Voluntary Hospitals in New York City," American Journal of Public Health 62 (October 1972), pp. 1370-1378.

26. Lowell Eleizer Bellin, "How to Make Ambulatory Care Start Ambulating," presented at the Joint Workshop, sponsored by the AHA and ADAC, Cherry Hill, Pa., November, 1971, p. 11.

27. See Gabriel A. Almond and G. Bingham Powell Jr, Comparative Politics: A Developmental Approach (Boston: Little, Brown, & Co. 1966).

28. For an examination of some of the pros and cons of existing prepaid programs such as Kaiser-Permanente and HIP see Merwyn R. Grunlick, "The Impact of Prepaid Group Practice on American Medical Care: A Critical Evaluation," The Annals of the American Academy of Political and Social Science, The Nation's Health: Some Issues, January 1972, pp. 100-113.

29. For additional discussion see Etzioni, The Active Society, chap. 20.

30. On the different types of systems that emerge, see Edward W. Lehman, "Control, Coordination and Crisis: Inter-Organizational Relations in the Health Field," Center for Policy Research Monograph, 1973.

31. James F. Blumstein and Michael Zubkoff, "Perspectives on Government Policy in the Health Sector," Milbank Memorial Fund Quarterly, Summer 1973, p. 398.

32. Ibid., 399-400.

33. Ibid., p. 400.

TABLE A-1

Utilization Trends, 1946-72

	1946	1972	Percent Change 1946-72
Population (000,000)	142	208	+47
Hospitals (total)	6,125	7,061	+15
Beds (000)	1,436	1,550	+8
Admissions (000)	15,675	33,265	+112
Outpatient Visits (000)	99,382	219,182	+121
Federal			
Hospitals	404	401	-1
Beds (000)	236	143	-39
Admissions (000)	1,593	1,770	+11
Outpatient Visits (000)	25,968	46,095	+78
Nongovernmental, Not-for-Profit			
Hospitals	2,584	3,326	+29
Beds (000)	301	617	+105
Admissions (000)	9,554	21,875	+129
Outpatient visits (000)	45,921	112,039	+144
For Profit			
Hospitals	1,076	738	-31
Beds (000)	39	57	+46
Admissions (000)	1,408	2,161	+54
Outpatient visits (000)	3,084	7,842	+154
State and Local			
Hospitals	785	1,779	+127
Beds (000)	133	209	+57
Admissions (000)	2,694	6,741	+150
Outpatient visits (000)	21,722	47,103	+117
Percent of Total Short-term Hospitals			
Federal	7	6	
Nongovernmental	42	47	
For profit	18	10	
State and Local	13	25	
Beds			
Federal	16	26	
Nongovernmental	21	40	
For profit	3	4	
State and Local	9	14	
Admissions			
Federal	10	5	
Nongovernmental	61	66	
For profit	9	7	
State and Local	17	20	
Outpatient Visits (1962-1972)			
Federal	26	21	
Nongovernmental	46	51	
For profit	3	4	
State and Local	22	22	

Note: Outpatient visits are for 1962.

Source: The 1973 AHA Guide to the Health Care Field, Table 1; and Statistical Abstract of the United States, 1972. (Nonfederal/Psychiatric, Nonfederal Tuberculosis and Nonfederal Long-Term General and Other Special Hospitals excluded. Also excluded are non-AHA registered and Osteopathic hospitals.)

TABLE A-2

Hospital Approvals and Affiliations, 1972

	All Hospitals		Nongovernmental Not-for-Profit		Federal		State and Local		Proprietary	
	Number	Percent	Number	Percent	Number	Percent	Number	Percent	Number	Percent
Total	7,061	100	3,326	100	401	100	1,779	100	738	100
Accreditation (A-1)	5,069	72	2,782	84	346	86	1,015	57	420	57
Cancer Program (A-2)	805	11	553	17	110	27	129	7	7	*
Residency (A-3)	1,203	17	709	21	140	35	160	9	7	*
Internship (A-4)	784	11	582	17	66	16	131	7	3	*
Medical School Affiliation (A-5)	621	9	354	11	92	23	110	6	3	*
Professional Nursing School (A-6)	486	7	416	13	2	*	50	3	6	*
Council of Teaching Hospitals (A-8)	400	6	239	7	70	17	84	5	1	*
Blue Cross Participation (A-9)	5,482	78	3,123	94	2	*	1,551	87	638	86
Medicare Certification (A-10)	5,981	85	3,176	95	5	*	1,667	94	627	85

*Less than 1 percent.

Source: Hospital Statistics, 1972 (Chicago: American Hospital Association, 1973), Table IIA, p. 200; definitions of approvals, p. 197.

STATEMENT ON A PATIENT'S
BILL OF RIGHTS
AFFIRMED BY THE BOARD OF TRUSTEES OF THE
AMERICAN HOSPITAL ASSOCIATION, NOVEMBER 17, 1972

The American Hospital Association presents a Patient's Bill of Rights with the expectation that observance of these rights will contribute to more effective patient care and greater satisfaction for the patient, his physician, and the hospital organization. Further, the Association presents these rights in the expectation that they will be supported by the hospital on behalf of its patients, as an integral part of the healing process. It is recognized that a personal relationship between the physician and the patient is essential for the provision of proper medical care. The traditional physician-patient relationship takes on a new dimension when care is rendered within an organization structure. Legal precedent has established that the institution itself also has a responsibility to the patient. It is in recognition of these factors that these rights are affirmed.

1. The patient has the right to considerate and respectful care.

2. The patient has the right to obtain from his physician complete current information concerning his diagnosis, treatment, and prognosis in terms the patient can be reasonably expected to understand. When it is not medically advisable to give such information to the patient, the information should be made available to an appropriate person in his behalf. He has the right to know, by name, the physician responsible for coordinating his care.

3. The patient has the right to receive from his physician information necessary to give informed consent prior to the start of any procedure and/or treatment. Except in emergencies, such information for informed consent should include but not necessarily be limited to the specific procedure and/or treatment, the medically significant risks involved, and the probable duration of incapacitation. Where medically significant alternatives for care or treatment exist, or when the patient requests information concerning medical alternatives, the patient has the right to such information. The patient also has the right to know the name of the person responsible for the procedures and/or treatment.

6. The patient has the right to expect that all communications and records pertaining to his care should be treated as confidential.

7. The patient has the right to expect that within its capacity a hospital must make reasonable response to the request of a patient for services. The hospital must provide evaluation, service, and/or referral as indicated by the urgency of the case. When medically permissible, a patient may be transferred to another facility only after he has received complete information and explanation concerning the needs for and alternatives to such a transfer. The institution to which the patient is to be transferred must first have accepted the patient for transfer.

8. The patient has the right to obtain information as to any relationship of his hospital to other health care and educational institutions insofar as his care is concerned. The patient has the right to obtain information as to the existence of any professional relationship among individuals, by name, who are treating him.

9. The patient has the right to be advised if the hospital proposes to engage in or perform human experimentation affecting his care or treatment. The patient has the right to refuse to participate in such research projects.

10. The patient has the right to expect reasonable continuity of care. He has the right to know in advance what appointment times and physicians are available and where. The patient has the right to expect that the hospital will provide a mechanism whereby he is informed by his physician or a delegate of the physician of the patient's continuing health care requirements following discharge.

11. The patient has the right to examine and receive an explanation of his bill regardless of source of payment.

12. The patient has the right to know what hospital rules and regulations apply to his conduct as a patient.

No catalog of rights can guarantee for the patient the kind of treatment he has a right to expect. A hospital has many functions to perform, including the prevention and treatment of disease, the education of both health professionals and patients, and the conduct of clinical research. All these activities must be conducted with an overriding concern for the patient, and, above all, the recognition of his dignity as a human being. Success in achieving this recognition assures success in the defense of the rights of the patient.

4. The patient has the right to refuse treatment to the extent permitted by law and to be informed of the medical consequences of his action.

5. The patient has the right to every consideration of his privacy concerning his own medical care program. Case discussion, consultation, examination, and treatment are confidential and should be conducted discreetly. Those not directly involved in his care must have the permission of the patient to be present.

TABLE B-1

VA Health Care Services, 1972-73

Item	Fiscal Year		Percent Change
	1973	1972	
Facilities operating at end of year			
Hospitals	169	167	+1.2
Domiciliaries	18	18	-
Outpatient clinics	206	203	+1.5
Nursing home units	82	77	+6.5
Restoration centers	0	8	-
Employment (net full-time equivalent)	161,250	153,031	+5.4
Operating costs (millions)	$2,661.7	$2,374.2	+12.1
Medical care	2,553.9	2,277.4	+12.1
Research	78.6	69.0	+13.9
Other	29.2	27.6	+5.8
Patients treated	1,082,476	944,189	+14.7
VA and other hospitals	1,014,383	876,274	+15.8
Other facilities	68,093	67,915	+0.3
Average daily patient census	115,170	113,905	+1.1
VA and other hospitals	84,556	83,185	+1.7
Other facilities	30,614	30,720	-0.3
Outpatient medical visits	10,858,491	9,526,881	+14.0
VA staff	9,165.094	7,930,080	+15.6
Fee-basis	1,693,397	1,596,801	+6.1
Outpatient dental examinations	227,777	256,738	-11.3
VA staff	114,199	142,919	-20.1
Fee-basis (net authorizations)	113,578	113,819	-0.2
Outpatient dental treatment cases			
Completed	248,388	248,692	-0.1
VA staff	82,916	82,873	+0.1
Fee-basis (net authorizations)	165,472	165,819	-0.2
Prescriptions filled (thousands)	21,400	16,706	+28.1
Specialized medical units	1,224	968	+26.5

Source: Veterans Administration, Annual Report, 1973, p. 9.

147

TABLE B-2

List of Reports Required By Law To Be Filed By VA Hospitals
(3/28/74 Request from CENTER FOR POLICY RESEARCH, INC.)

RCS No.	Title	Requiring Instructions
A-12	Annual Report of Position Reviews and Comparative Average Salaries and Grades	P. L. 253, 82nd Cong. 65 Stat. 757 Sec. 1310
MAS 2	Contract Printing Report, JCP Form No. 2	44 U.S.C. 501-502
MAS 4	Inventory of Stored Equipment – Annual JCP Form No. 6	44 U.S.C. 501-502
10-251	Annual Report by Administrator of Veterans Affairs on Sharing Medical Resources and the Exchange of Medical Information	38 U.S.C. 5057
None	Report to Senate and House Committees on Agriculture of dairy products acquired from the Commodity Credit Corporation for use in Veterans' Administration hospitals	7 U.S.C. 1446a (a)
None	Report (whenever violation occurs) of expenditure or obligation in excess of appropriation or apportionment	31 U.S.C. 665 (i) (2)

Source: Personal Communication from Office of Controller, Reports and Statistics Service, Veterans Administration.

148

TABLE C-1

Hospital Utilization, 1972 Distribution by Type and Control

Classification	Percent Distribution[a]			
	Hospitals	Beds	Admissions	Outpatient Visits
Short–Term General	100	100	100	100
Nongovernmental, not–for–profit	54	64	68	53
For profit	12	6	7	4
Federal government	6	9	5	21
Local government	27	19	19	17
State government	2	3	2	6
Short–Term Psychiatric	100	100	100	100
Nongovernmental, not–for–profit	33	28	30	23
For profit	47	31	36	12
Federal government	0	0	0	0
Local government	4	10	7	16
State government	17	31	27	27
All Other[b]	100	100	100	100
Nongovernmental, not–for–profit	62	62	71	62
For profit	27	13	15	13
Federal government	(3)	5	1	3
Local government	5	10	6	7
State government	5	9	6	15
Long–Term General	100	100	100	100
Nongovernmental, not–for–profit	2	(c)	(c)	0
For profit	4	1	1	1
Federal government	59	84	93	87
Local government	20	6	3	3
State government	16	8	3	9

(continued)

149

(Table C-1 continued)

Classification	Percent Distribution[a]			
	Hospitals	Beds	Admissions	Outpatient Visits
Long-Term Psychiatric	100	100	100	100
Nongovernmental, not-for-profit	11	1	4	9
For profit	11	1	4	3
Federal government	7	7	14	22
Local government	4	3	2	4
State government	69	88	77	62
Long-Term Tuberculosis and Other Respiratory	100	100	100	100
Nongovernmental, not-for-profit	7	3	3	1
For profit	0	0	0	0
Federal government	0	0	0	0
Local government	35	21	19	71
State government	58	76	78	27
Long-Term Other	100	100	100	100
Nongovernmental, not-for-profit	51	27	39	47
For profit	4	1	3	1
Federal government	1	2	2	1
Local government	25	44	38	31
State government	19	25	18	19

aMay not add to 100 due to rounding.
bIncludes maternity, eye, ear, nose, and throat and other special units.
cLess than 1 percent.

Source: Hospital Statistics, 1972 (Chicago: American Hospital Association, 1973), Table 2, pp. 22-5

TABLE C-2

Distribution of Emergency Room and Outpatient Visits, New York City, 1972

Control Type	Number of Hospitals	Bed Complement	Emergency Room Visits	Outpatient Visits
Voluntary	72	28,119	1,540,133	3,356,503
Municipal	18	14,941	1,670,375	3,295,410
Proprietary	35	5,087	76,423	0
State	10	8,055	935[a]	55,302[a]
Total	135	56,272	3,287,866	6,707,215

Percent Distribution

Voluntary	53	50	47	50
Municipal	13	27	51	49
Proprietary	26	9	2	0
State	7	14	[b]	[b]
Total	100	100	100	100

[a]Data for one state hospital only.

[b]Less than 1 percent, total rounded.

Source: Hospitals and Related Facilities in Southern New York, 1973, Health and Hospital Planning Council of Southern New York, Inc., p. 5; Emergency Room and Outpatient Data by personal communication to author.

The Article 28 Story

LANDMARK IN HEALTH FACILITY PLANNING

Article 28

. . . In order to provide for the protection and promotion of the Health of the inhabitants of the state . . . the Department of Health shall have the central comprehensive responsibility for the development and administration of the state's policy with respect to hospitals and related services, and all public and private institutions, whether state, county, municipal, incorporated or not incorporated, serving principally as facilities for the prevention, diagnosis or treatment of human diseases, pain, injury, deformity or physical condition. . . .

Declaration of Policy
Article 28 of the Public Health Law

Purpose of the Program

With passage of Article 28 of the Public Health Law in 1965, New York became the first state to develop a program of mandatory health facility planning directed toward

- Controlling spiraling health care costs
- Preventing unnecessary construction and duplication of services
- Ensuring quality control over health facility operation
- Providing capital funding to assist the development of needed health facilities.

Published by New York State Department of Health, Hollis S. Ingraham, M.D., Commissioner (no date).

The program was initiated at Governor Rockefeller's request, following an in-depth study of health facility economies carried out by the Governor's Committee on Hospital Costs. This committee's report showed that random, unplanned development of health care facilities, which existed up to that time not only in New York State but throughout the country, had resulted in costly duplication of services and marked disparity in the availability and quality of health care in different geographical locations across the State.

Article 28, and subsequent amendments to that law, is the legislation enacted to correct such shortcomings by implementing over 50 recommendations proposed by the Committee toward improving health care services in New York State.

Scope of the Program

Article 28 assigns the State Health Department central responsibility for coordinating the development of health care facilities and ensuring the uniform quality of health care services throughout the State.

To carry out this broad responsibility, the Department has direct authority over every health care facility in the State, with the exception of federal hospitals and those providing mainly mental health services. This authority extends not only to hospitals and nursing homes, but to health related facilities, ambulatory care facilities, clinics and any and all public or private institutions providing diagnosis or treatment for humaphysical conditions.

The Department sets standards and exercises the right of regular inspection, audit and review over every aspect of health facility planning, construction, and operation. In effect, without Health Department approval new facilities may not be established and existing facilities may not continue to operate in New York State.

How the Program Works

Establishment of New Facilities

Any individual or group proposing to establish a new health care facility in New York State must obtain the prior approval of the State Public Health Council—a governor-appointed advisory body, composed of the State Health Commissioner and 14 members representing consumer, professional and statewide health interests.

In arriving at its decision, the Public Health Council receives and independent assessment of the proposal from:

- The State Hospital Review and Planning Council
- The Regional Planning Council and/or Areawide Health Planning Agency in whose area the project will be located
- The staff of the State Health Department.

Final approval is granted only when the Public Health Council is satisfied that all four of the primary criteria for approval are met.

Facility Construction or Renovation

Prior approval of the State Health Commissioner is required for construction of a new health facility or modernization, replacement or renovation of any existing facility.

In arriving at his decision, the Commissioner reviews the proposal in terms of the four main approval criteria and receives the recommendations of both the statewide and appropriate regional planning councils.

A detailed evaluation of the proposal is also made by the State Health Department's specialized architectural and engineering staff to assure that

- The facility conforms to all construction standards under the State Hospital Code
- All possible construction and design economies are incorporated to keep costs at a minimum
- The capacity of the facility will meet current and projected needs of the population it is meant to serve.

Final approval is predicated on the project's compliance with current land use, building code and zoning ordinances in the city, county or locality in which it will be situated.

Health Services

The State Health Commissioner must also approve the complete program of services proposed for a new health facility, as well as any addition, deletion or change in the services provided by an existing facility.

The Commissioner similarly reviews each proposal in terms of the established approval criteria and receives the recommendations of both the statewide and regional planning councils.

Criteria for Approval

At each stage in the approval process, the designated reviewing bodies evaluate the proposal in terms of the following criteria and recommend approval or disapproval according to their findings:

1. Does a public need exist for the facility or service in the time, place and circumstances proposed by the sponsors?
2. Do the sponsors have adequate character and competence to operate such a facility?
3. Is sufficient financing available for creation of the proposed program of services?
4. Will the cost for such services be reasonable in terms of the economic market to be served?

Financing of Facility Construction and Improvement

New York State provides low-cost, long-term mortgage loans for construction and modernization of needed public or non-profit health facilities. These funds, totaling approximately $5.8 billion, are raised through the sale of bonds by the State Housing Finance Agency and are available for projects that have received the approval of the State Health Commissioner.

Certification and Licensing

The State Health Commissioner has the power to inquire into any aspect of health facility operation and to conduct regular inspections of all facilities to assure the fitness and adequacy of the premises, equipment, personnel, rules and by-laws, standards of care, system of accounts and records, and financial resources.

Based on these findings, the Commissioner may continue to license the facility or revoke or suspend its right to operate in New York State.

A 1970 amendment to the law also gave the Commissioner authority to monitor health facility costs and charges and to set rates for Medicaid and Blue Cross reimbursement.

Right of Hearing

Should the State Health Commissioner or Public Health Council propose disapproval of a project, the sponsor is afforded the opportunity for a public hearing where he may present supporting arguments before an independent hearing officer.

REVIEW AND APPROVAL PROCEDURE

Establishment and Construction
of a New Health Facility

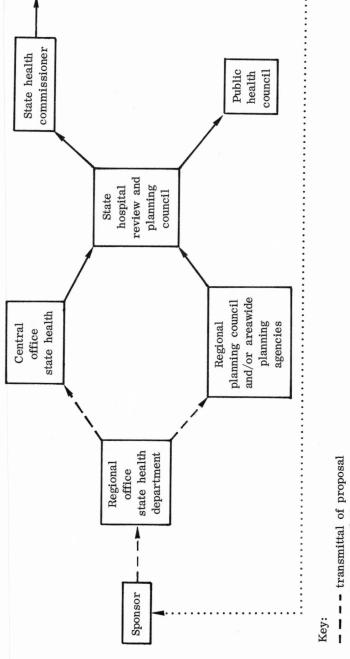

Key:
— — — transmittal of proposal
———— recommendation
·········· final decision

TABLE D-1

Percent Distribution of Nursing Care and Related Homes, 1971

Ownership	Total Homes	Nursing Care	With nursing	Without nursing	Domiciliary care
HOMES					
Total Homes	100	100	100	100	100
Government	6	6	6	4	3
federal	*	*	*	*	1
state-local	5	6	5	4	2
Proprietary	77	77	64	86	80
Nonprofit	16	15	28	9	15
church	4	3	8	1	2
other	12	11	20	7	12
BEDS					
Total Beds	100	100	100	100	100
Government	10	9	12	8	4
federal	*	*	1	1	2
state-local	9	9	10	6	1
Proprietary	67	72	38	74	43
Nonprofit	22	17	49	16	52
church	6	4	17	4	22
other	16	12	32	12	29

*Less than 1 percent.

Note: Totals rounded.

Source: Data from Health Resources Statistics, 1972-73, Table 223, p. 396, Department of Health, Education, and Welfare.

The Public Health Council will similarly grant a hearing to the State Hospital Review and Planning Council or the regional planning councils if it intends to act contrary to their recommendations.

The right of a public hearing is also provided before revocation or suspension of a facility's operating license.

This sytem of checks and balances ensures that all factors are carefully weighed, all points of view represented and arbitrary decisions affecting the State's health care services avoided.

Results of the Program

New York State's program of mandatory health facility planning went into effect in February 1966.

Based on the results of the first six years of the program, it is estimated that a projected statewide need for 87,000 general care beds and 117,000 long-term-care beds of high quality will be fully met by 1977.

During the first six years, the State Health Department received and processed over 3,400 applications seeking permission to establish 136,000 beds and 600 ambulatory care projects.

Of that total, the Department approved proposals to add over 83,000 beds. For various reasons, primarily a considered lack of need, the Department disapproved construction of 51,000 beds—thus saving approximately $1.6 billion in capital costs and $738 million annually in unnecessary operating costs.

Since the law took effect, 28 non-conforming hospitals and 281 non-conforming nursing homes have been closed. Nearly 2,000 maternity beds in hospitals throughout the State have been closed or converted to other, more needed, uses.

In the two years in which the Health Department has had authority to monitor costs and charges, the rate of increase in hospital and nursing home costs has been significantly slowed. Within one year the increase in Medicaid rates declined from 19.1 percent (in 1970) to 10.2 percent (in 1971). In some areas of the State this rate dropped to 5 percent in 1972.

In general, a comparison of New York's present health care picture with that of the nation as a whole, where development has been largely uncontrolled over the same period, shows that the State's mandatory health facility planning program has resulted in

- Construction of fewer, larger and more efficient health facilities, with a simultaneous reduction in the number of small inefficient in-patient facilities

- Improved use rates by the population and more efficient levels levels of occupancy
- Improved availability, quality of care and structural conformity in all facilities throughout the State.

PATIENT GRIEVANCE REPORT

Liery Wynn, Health Advocate

The Center's administration has adopted an unusually demo-
cratic attitude on the delivery of health care, facilitating the advocacy
program from which patients' grievance procedure originated. The
grievance procedure was developed and adopted as Health Center
policy in July 1970.

Traditionally, health facilities are not interested in dealing
with the rights or the feelings of the patients they serve. At MLK we
feel that being sensitive to the emotional needs and desires of a patient
is as much an integral part of the treatment plan as the actual pre-
scribing of medicine.

The grievance procedure was developed mainly to deal with the
humane—rather than the legal—rights of a patient. This is not to say
that the legal rights are not important. Realizing that a patient's
legal rights are guaranteed in the court system, we wanted to deal
with those rights that a patient could not take to court, for example,
an employee's shouting at a patient.

We have defined and attempted to insure the following rights of
patients: the right to courtesy and respect; the right to refuse treatment; the right to privacy, for example, one should not be questioned
about coverage under Medicaid in public; the right to choose time for
appointments; the right to transportation to and from the Center when
disabled; the right to have help in applying for Medicaid; and the right
to informed consent regarding the exchange of information between
the Health Center and other agencies, for example, schools and
referrals. These are all clearly delineated in The Patients' Rights
Manual which was developed by the Center staff.

The grievance procedure was designed to resolve problems in
the quickest way possible. First the patient is urged to speak with

From Sixth Report, Dr. Martin Luther King Jr. Health Center,
January 1972—July 1973, pp. 220-221.

any employee that he feels has abridged his rights as soon as it happens. If this proves unsatisfactory, the patient can then fill out a complaint form or call the patient advocate who is responsible for handling such situations.

Complaint Procedure

When contacted, the patient advocate has a four-stage procedure to follow in working to resolve the complaint.

Stage 1. The patient advocate receives or fills out a complaint form, which includes a narrative of the complaint and name of the staff member involved. After he sends copies to all persons who will have a role in the procedure, the patient advocate meets with the staff member who was involved in the incident. Seventy-five percent of complaints are resolved at this level.

Stage 2. If this meeting does not resolve the issue, the patient advocate takes the complaint to the staff member's supervisor. The supervisor must report his decision and action on the matter within five days to the patient advocate, who relays the information to the patient. Ten percent of complaints are resolved here.

Stage 3. If the patient is still dissatisfied, the patient advocate schedules a conference for the client, the staff person involved and his representative, the department head or supervisor and the advocate. Ten percent of complaints are settled here.

Stage 4. If the issues are not resolved at this stage, it is likely that several patients have made similar complaints about the individual or situation. In this case, the patient advocate recommends changes to the Project Director and the Community Advisory Board. Five percent of complaints reach this level.

GUIDE TO THE BEST HEALTH CARE FOR YOUR MONEY

I. INTRODUCTION

The State has prepared this health consumer's Guide to the Best Health Care for Your Money to provide the public with general information about your rights as a patient, to help you identify better quality health services, to help you direct your complaints and dissatisfaction to the right place and, hopefully, to get you a little bit more for the health dollar you spend.

People expect to get something for their money when they buy a new car, or invest in an expensive appliance. But they tend to be less critical of the health care they receive for the money they spend. If you are willing to speak up, be interested in your care, ask the right questions, and understand that buying health care is basically the same as buying a refrigerator or car, you may save money and get better care.

II. Your Rights as a Patient

Most people do not know that even as patients they have rights. Recently, an increased consumer awareness about Patient Rights has developed. The American Hospital Association has prepared a bill of rights for use by member hospitals. You can get a copy of this by writing to the AHA, 840 North Lake Shore Drive, Chicago, Illinois, 60611. Some of these rights have bases in law; some in professional ethics; and some in the moral code of our society. They are also based on the fact that you are not a guest in a hospital, nor is your doctor treating you for nothing. Patients are clients who are paying for a professional service. When you are sick or disabled, and under

---

Reprinted with permission from The Cost of Health Care in New York State, A Six Month Interim Report prepared by The Temporary State Commission on Living Costs and the Economy, April 1974.

someone else's care, you do have rights; it is up to you to make sure
that these rights are honored.

- Patients have a right to know who is treating them, what
  the treatment is, why that method of treatment is being
  used, the effects, possible side effects, alternatives to
  this treatment and its costs. Ask questions about your
  illness. You are entitled to receive clear, precise
  answers in easy to understand terms. You have a right
  to know what you are paying for.
- Patients do not have to sign anything but may be requested
  to complete admitting forms, insurance forms and consent
  forms among others. Patients have a right to know what
  these forms are about, what they mean, and understand
  their contents before they are signed.
- Health institutions have ways to handle patient complaints
  and grievances. Ask about these complaint procedures.
  Know how to use them. Grievance mechanisms aren't
  always an effective route for solving a problem. When
  you make inquiries, ask nurses, social workers, etc.,
  who handles the complaints and whether they are usually
  resolved.
- Patients have a right to high quality care at the lowest
  possible cost. As tax payers and the ultimate payers
  for all medical care, research and training, you have
  a right to information about health care facilities and
  the people involved in providing health services.
- Patients have a right to receive care with respect, understanding and compassion.

It isn't always easy to get satisfaction when you have a problem
or complaint. The fact that you should be treated in a certain way does
not mean that you will be. There may even be instances when you
feel that you have not been treated fairly despite all your efforts. We
want to emphasize, however, that it is important for all patients to
expect their rights to be respected and act accordingly. Otherwise,
the recent efforts toward consumer power in the health field which
have resulted in general recognition of Patients' Rights will be in
vain.

III. Myths and Facts About Health Care

Situation 1: Choosing a Hospital

You go to your family doctor and are told that you must be admitted to a hospital. Although your illness is not serious, you should
not wait the many weeks it will take to be admitted to hospital "A"
(the better hospital). Your doctor reassures you that he would not
admit you to hospital 'B' (the not-so-good hospital) unless he was sure
that they could adequately treat your illness. You agree to be admitted
to hospital "B" immediately.
Myth: Only your doctor can admit you to Hospital A.
Fact: Any doctor on a Hospital A's staff can admit you to that hospital.
      The truth is, in case of serious illness, you can be admitted to
      the hospital of your choice by selecting the right doctor; and
      the right doctor is a qualified or board certified specialist
      who has admitting privileges at that hospital. Ask your
      physicians about their admitting privileges and where
      they hospitalize most of their patients.
      If you do not feel confident about the hospital where your doctor
plans to admit you, find yourself another doctor. This can be done
easily enough. Call the hospital where you want to be admitted and ask
for the names of several staff doctors (in the specialty that you need).
If your case is urgent, your doctor should be fighting to get you into
the better hospital. It is your decision to choose the hospital you will
be admitted to. Ask your family doctor where his or her family members go when they are as ill as you.

Situation 2: Knowing Your Insurance Coverage

You have just been hired by company X. Although your hospital
and medical insurance were described to you, you are not quite sure
what is covered and not covered. You go into the Personnel Department
and ask them about your benefits and they answer your questions, but
cannot provide any written material to you.
Myth: The Company pays for it, so whatever they pay for, you are
      ahead.
Fact: Your fringe benefits, including hospital and medical care in-
      surance, are part of a total package for which you pay with your
work. You have a right to know what your employee insurance covers.
As an employee, you have a legal right to receive a copy of your hospital and medical insurance policy. Do not wait until you or a member
becomes ill to find out that your policy is filled with loopholes and
small print. Find out from your employer the specific terms covered
and not covered, who is covered, the amounts of deductibles and

and <u>co-insurance</u> that you are responsible for, the <u>date</u> the insurance begins, the conditions under which it continues and if it may be discontinued under any conditions. Once you have itemized the types of hospital and medical care not covered, you may wish to purchase additional health insurance through your employer, if available, or seek additional insurance from an outside source. A thorough understanding of your insurance policy will allow you to make an intelligent decision about the type of insurance that you specifically need to fill the gaps in your present insurance policy. Any unanswered questions should be sent to the Superintendent of Insurance, New York State Department of Insurance, 123 William Street, New York, New York 10038.

Situation 3: Paying for What You Get

You receive an itemized bill for hospitalization, services rendered on an outpatient basis or in a doctor's office. Your bill includes certain tests that you weren't aware of. Since they are covered by your insurance, you do not worry about whether or not they are legitimately charged to you.

<u>Myth</u>: Since your insurance covers the cost of the tests, you should not make a big deal about the fact that you don't think the tests were ever done.

<u>Fact</u>: Every item on your bill, including expenses for which you are not directly responsible, contributes to the cost of health care in some way. You may feel it in future premium increase or a decrease in benefits. For every extra dollar your insurance company has to pay out, you will eventually feel the inflationary impact. So it is in your interest to be as certain as possible that you are only charged for what you get.

IV. Your Doctor

Your Attitude

One of the most important decisions you will make about medical care is your choice of a personal physician. Most people, so the story goes, are not qualified to judge the competency and skill of physicians. The lack of confidence people feel about their ability to judge a physician can create an attitude of fear or restraint. You should never be afraid to ask direct questions. Always remember that it is <u>your health</u> which is at stake. Ask about your care, ask about fees, and make any objections known.

Choosing Your Doctor

1. Ask your friends or relatives to recommend a doctor they like and respect. Most people choose their doctors this way. If you use this method, be sure to ask why they like and respect the doctor they recommend. You may want to consult the Directory of New York State Physicians for further information before making a decision. Most likely you won't find out about professional credentials through friends, and this could be important information. However, you can't find out about the attitude of the physican towards patients through a Directory. Both are important.

2. Consult the directory of New York State physicians published annually by the New York State Medical Society. This directory lists medical school background and training, hospital affiliations, teaching positions, memberships in professional associations. This may be of assistance in determining whether or not you want to follow the suggested choice of the friend or relative. You can find this directory in a public or medical school library.

3. Ask a physician or a local hospital for a list of physicians.

4. Choosing a specialist:
    (a) Look for Board Certification (the doctor has passed professionally established tests in his specialty). Look in directory or on the wall of the doctor's office for a certificate.
    (b) Look for admitting privileges at hospitals which keep up with the latest medical advances: teaching hospitals are usually a good bet.
    (c) There is a Directory of Medical Specialists which you can also consult at the public library or a medical school library.

Your First Visit (or Interviewing Your Physician-To-Be)

Ask about insurance coverage, particpation in medical insurance plans like Blue Shield, Group Health Insurance, labor-management health and welfare funds, or the Health Insurance Plan of Greater New York. If you are over 65, ask if the physician accepts Medicare allowables.

Observe the physician's attitude toward you. Does he or she answer questions respectfully and openly? Do you feel comfortable with the physician?

Discuss fees openly. Remember, you are paying for a service: would you want to employ someone without knowing what you were going to have to pay them? Ask the cost of an office visit. If the price is unusually high, this may be a crucial factor in your decision.

Ask about what is included in the visit fee. Are lab tests included?
How much will they cost?

Ask the doctor if he will prescribe drugs by their generic name.
The generic name is an adopted chemical name used by pharmacists,
as opposed to a patented name used by a company that manufactures
a given drug. Generics are generally agreed to be equally as effective
as brand names. Ordering drugs by generic name rather than brand
name will save you money.

<u>Pre-paid Group Practice Plans</u>

Over the last thirty years, several major pre-paid group
practice plans have been developed to offer an alternative to the
customary fee-for-service solo practice. This is the professional
term for a doctor practicing privately. Pre-paid group practice like
private practice has its assets and weaknesses. Pre-paid group
practices potentially can provide good medical care at a reasonable
cost, reduce unnecessary surgery and provide an alternative to
fragmented services with doctor, laboratory and hospital facilities
in separate places. In group practice, several physicians with
various specialties work under one roof with additional services such
as x-ray and laboratory facilities. The patient pays a fixed monthly
fee to the organization and upon payment is automatically covered for
most medical and surgical services, laboratory work and other
services, both in-hospital and on an ambulatory or out-patient basis.

Potential disadvantages of group practice are lack of continuity
of service and an impersonal doctor-patient relationship. The administrative efficiency of group practices can also vary from one to
another, and not all are oriented toward saving money for the patient.

<u>Employee or Union Health Centers</u>

Some people in this State have access to health centers through
their employers or unions. Many of these centers provide high quality
care and many, although convenient, are not used to full capacity.
You should take advantage of these health centers which are available
at no cost or a reduced cost to the member or employee. Remember
to be as critical of these services as any other. They should meet
the same standards already discussed. Although they may be "no
cost" or reduced cost, persons eligible for these services have paid
by their labor and have a right to evaluate, criticize and push for
change.

V. Out-Patient Department—The New Family Physician

For many New York State residents, the local community hospital is the main source of medical care. Health consumers who use out-patient department should know that they have rights as ambulatory patients which parallel those they have as in-patients. These include the right to humane and dignified treatment, the right to ask questions about fees and the right to receive an itemized bill. Some out-patient departments have teaching programs for recently licensed doctors and medical students. Concerned new doctors and medical students can bring the best of modern medicine to out-patients. They can also bring the worst. You should be aware of this. A patient has the right to ask what rank the doctor treating him or her has (medical student, intern, resident, or attending physician). A patient can refuse treatment from non-M.D.s.

Ideally, there should be an ombudsman, patient coordinator or advocate to assist out-patients. A department of social services should be available to anyone requesting assistance. There should be translators to facilitate communication between doctor and patient. Most out-patient departments participate in Medicare and Medicaid programs and will assist the patient in the paperwork and completion of forms required.

The following are a few questions by which you can rate your hospital out-patient department. The answer in each case should be "yes."

Checklist for Quality Outpatient Care:

1. Do you feel that the doctor is really interested in finding out what is wrong with you?
2. Does the out-patient department extend the right of a primary physician to out-patients? If this is hospital policy, demand that you have one.
3. Did the doctor ask you for your complete medical history, including family tendencies and allergic reactions?
4. Does your doctor tell you where to get medical care when the center is closed?
5. Are you told why you have to return to the center, or why you have to take ordered lab and x-ray tests?
6. Does the doctor explain the nature and purpose of any prescription he or she gives you?
7. For women: Does the doctor give you a PAP test and a breast examination at your yearly physical?
8. Are questions answered to your satisfaction?

9.   Are you treated respectfully?

VI. The Hospital

Is the hospital properly licensed and does it meet State and local health code regulations? This can usually be confirmed if the hospital has a certificate of occupancy posted in a conspicuous location in the hospital. Under Federal Law, inspection reports on hospitals participating in the Medicare program are made available to the public at local Social Security Administration offices.

Is the hospital accredited by the Joint Commission on the Accreditation of Hospitals? Most of the nation's general hospitals are accredited by this private, non-profit organization. Accreditation by the JCAH means that the hospital has measured up to national standards established by this group. It should be known, however, that these standards are very broad and basic. JCAH accreditation is granted to almost every hospital. The accreditation does not mean necessarily that the hospital is top notch. Refusal of accreditation, on the contrary, may mean that the hospital is very poor.

Does the hospital have approved teaching programs?

Teaching hospitals have a potential for bringing modern medicine to the bed of the patient. Some health professionals believe the quality of care is better in teaching hospitals.

Who controls or owns the hospital?

Some hospitals are operated to make a profit and are known as proprietary hospitals. These institutions provide services that generally do not require the more sophisticated equipment or staff. However, they can provide, in many cases, more than adequate care for routine medical-surgical problems.

Patients have the right to enter a hospital when medically indicated without regard to race, sex or method of payment; it is important to know this, because some hospitals have been known to turning patients away for lacking insurance coverage. Patients also have a right to deny treatment as permitted by law, to leave the hospital, and to die. Patients must give informed consent before being involved in research, undergoing surgery or receiving specialized diagnostic and therapeutic care that may have harmful side effects.

Prior to entering a hospital, you can determine certain conditions such as cleanliness, presence or lack of a patient coordinator, and concern with the rights of a patient by visiting the facility and asking questions. People who spend $50 a day to go to a resort hotel usually research what to expect in terms of quality of service; you should do at least as much prior to entering a hospital which may be charging up to $200 a day.

VII. Nursing Homes

Before making a final decision on a nursing home you <u>must</u> make a personal inspection of the premises. In fact, it is important to vist the home twice. From a formal tour and discussion with the administrators you will be able to determine such things as proper licensing, general cleanliness and physical comforts. A second, unannounced visit is important to determine attitude of staff towards patient, actual quality of food served, and atmosphere of the home. You will probably get a slightly different view when you visit the home informally.

Be sure to find out if the home has a current license from the State. The administrator should also have a current license from the State. Check to make sure the home is certified to participate in the Medicare and Medicaid programs. You can also check at your local Social Security-Medicare office for "Disclosure Form #2567" on a given nursing home. Federal law requires that this form be filed after a survey of the nursing home and that any significant deficiencies be listed.

During your visit to the home, you should ask patients, staff and administrator all the questions you wish to have answered. A checklist which may be helpful to you is included below:

1. Who provides medical care? How often is a patient seen? Are medical records kept and relatives notified of changes in patients' condition?
2. Is the nursing home near a hospital?
3. Is physical therapy available and how often?
4. Is the building well lit, free of hazards and fireproof?
5. Is the furniture secure and sturdy?
6. Is the home generally clean and free of unpleasant odors?
7. Are there handles in the hallways and grab-bars in the bathrooms?
8. How many beds are there to a room?
9. Are there frequent fire drills, posted emergency instructions, and clear stairways?
10. Is there a variety of high quality food? Are special diets provided? Is the kitchen clean?
11. Is food delivered to the patient's room?

12. Are the eating quarters and recreation areas attractive and well-kept?
13. Are there activities and special programs available?
14. Are there opportunities for religious observances?
15. Is the attitude of the staff humane and responsive to individual patients?
16. Do the staff members respond quicly to patient calls for assistance?
17. Is there a mechanism for people to properly voice their complaints?
18. Is an itemized bill provided on a regular basis?

VIII. Surgery

Surgery, no matter how simple, is a serious proposition. A moment of great concern comes when a family doctor tells a patient that surgery is needed. As a patient, your major concern is to ask one simple question: IS SURGERY NECESSARY? You have a right to know what options and alternatives are available to you and what will happen if you do not have surgery. You have a right to know how surgery will affect you and what your chances are for success. Before deciding upon surgery, you should seek a second opinion from an independently selected board certified physician. An independent second opinion is your best safeguard to avoid unnecessary surgery. In a few cases, a third opinion may be necessary. But the money spent to verify the need for surgery is money well spent.

If you make the decision to undergo surgery, you should make sure that the surgeon is certified by the appropriate American College of Surgeons. To find the right surgeon, consult the Directory of Medical Specialists or call the local County Medical Society (The American College of Osteopathic Surgeons can provide you with the same information for Osteopaths).

Ask your surgeon where he or she intends to hospitalize you and perform the surgery. Make sure the hospital meets the criteria listed in VI above. Be sure to ask your physician and surgeon about fees and participation in medical-surgical plans, to learn if they accept your insurance coverage.

IX. DENTISTRY

Dentistry is a problem to the health care consumer because it is generally extremely expensive and is not covered by most insurance policies. Below is a checklist to rate your dentist:

1.   Is your dentist concerned with protection-oriented dentistry, or with teaching you the best way to care for your teeth to avoid unnecessary visits to the dentist?

2.   Does your dentist answer your questions about fees and estimates?

3.   Does your dentist explain alternative treatments and possible complications of treatment?

4.   Is your dentist a jack-of-all-trades or does he or she feel free to send you to a dental specialist when needed?

5.   Does your dentist seem eager to cap teeth, pull teeth, or try expensive dental contraptions?

The clinics of dental schools often provide high quality dental care at low cost. Dental students under the supervision of a qualified dentist may treat you a little slower but the reduced cost and higher quality of care afforded by careful supervision may be a smart alternative to consider.

X. Where To Go With Complaints

If you have a complaint about a health care facility, the service you receive or what it costs you, there are a number of places you can voice your complaint. As you can see from the following 20-item list, there are appropriate places for different kinds of complaints. There are also back-up resources such as consumer and health advocacy groups and legal aid available if you do not obtain satisfaction elsewhere.

1.   Patient representative at the institution.

2.   The administrator of the facility concerned.

3.   Board of Directors or Owners of the institution.

4.   The patient's caseworker of the County Welfare Office if the patient is covered by Medicaid.

5.   The State Board responsible for licensing administrators (get address information from the Welfare Department).

6.   The State Medicaid Agency if the institution is certified for that program.

7.   The local Social Security District Office functions as a clearing house for nursing home and hospital complaints (Medicare).

8.   The State Health Department and the State Licensing Authority.

9.   State Department of Insurance (123 William Street, New York, N.Y. 10038).

10.   Your local Better Business Bureau and Chamber of Commerce.

11.   The Consumer Affairs Office if such an office has been established in your community.

12. Your local Hospital Association and Medical Society.
13. The Joint Commission on Accreditation of Hospitals (875 North Michigan Avenue, Chicago, Ill. 60611).
14. The American Nursing Home Association (Suite 607, 1025 Connecticut Avenue N.W., Washington, D.C. 20004) if the home is a member.
15. The American Association of Homes for the Aging (529 Fourteenth Street, N.W., Washington, D.C. 20004) if the home is a member.
16. The American College of Nursing Home Administrators (Suite 409, the Eig Building, 8641 Colesville Road, Silver Spring, Md. 20910) if the administrator is a member.
17. Your representatives in Congress and the Senate. Address: House of Representatives, Washington, D.C. 20515; United States Senate, Washington, D.C. 20510).
18. Your State and local elected representatives.
19. Health advocacy groups, or the community board of the hospital.
20. A reputable lawyer or Legal Aid Society.

Kaitz, Edward M., 12
Kellogg Foundation,(see
  Acknowledgments)
Kessler, Ronald, 103-104
Klarman, Herbert E., 11, 54, 56
Kristol, Irving, v

Lee, Philip, 41
Lehman, Edward W., 142
Leveson, Irving, 107
Lewis, Howard and Martha, 10
local health facilities, Chap. 3
  passim and 112-114
long term care facilities (see
  also extended care facilities,
  nursing homes), 73 et seq.
  and 114-115

Martin Luther King Jr. Health
  Center (MLK), 94, 130
Maryland (Secretary of Health
  and Mental Hygiene), 75
Master Facility Inventory
  (HEW), 74
McNerney, Walter, 108
Medicare and Medicaid (Titles
  18 and 19 of the Social Security
  Act): Medicare, 2, 57-58, 76,
  77, 81, 82, 93, 97; Medicaid,
  76, 77, 78, 79, 82, 93, 94,
  97, 109, 116
Medical Audit Committees, 35
medical staff, 6-7
medical staff organization, 69
Mendelson, Mary Adelaide, 80
Metcalf-McClosky Act (N.Y.), 75
Miami Veterans Administration
  Hospital, 40
Montefiore Hospital and Medical
  Center (N.Y.), 94
Morehead, Mildred A., 95, 96
Multipurpose Health Services
  Center (Watts), 91
Munk,(Michael and Ken Saffier),
  16

Musser, Marc J., 33-34

Nader, Ralph (Nader Report), 39,
  43, 44
Nassau County Medical Center
  (N.Y.), 104
National Academy of Engineering,
  20
National Council of Senior Citizens,
  83
Neighborhood Health Centers,(see
  Chap. 5 and 116)
Neighborhood Health Council, 89
New York City (municipal hospitals),
  50, 51-52
New York State Association for
  Retarded Children, 60
New York State Department of
  Mental Hygiene, 57, 59, 60
New York State, Public Health
  Council, 75
New York State Public Health Law,
  4, 57;(see also Appendix F,
  152)
New York State Temporary Com-
  mission on Living Costs and
  Economy (Stein Commission),
  58, 59, 104;(see also Appendix
  F, 152)
nursing homes (see also extended
  care facilities; long term care
  facilities), 73 et seq. and
  114-115

Office of Economic Opportunity
  (U.S.), 88
Office of Management and Budget
  (U.S.), 33, 35, 40
ombudsman, 83, 111
Ostow, Miriam (and Charles
  Brecher), 55, 87

patient advocates, 111, 130
Patient's Bill of Rights (AHA), 92,
  (see also Appendix A-3, 145)

ABOUT THE AUTHOR

HARRY I. GREENFIELD is Professor of Economics at Queens
College of the City University of New York and Senior Research
Associate at the Center For Policy Research Inc.

Dr. Greenfield has published in the field of general economics
as well as in the economics of health. Previous books include: Manpower and the Growth of Producer Services and Allied Health Manpower: Trends and Prospects, both by Columbia University Press,
and Hospital Efficiency and Public Policy, published by Praeger.
His articles and reviews have appeared in: Journal of the American
Medical Association; American Journal of Public Health; Bulletin of
the New York Academy of Medicine; Monthly Labor Review; Quarterly
Review of Economics and Business; The Financial Analysts Journal;
The Commercial and Financial Chronicle; and Computers and
Automation.

Dr. Greenfield holds a B.S.S. from City College of the City
University of New York and an M.A. and Ph.D. from Columbia
University.

RELATED TITLES
Published by
Praeger Special Studies

CHANGING THE MEDICAL CARE SYSTEM:
A Controlled Experiment in Comprehensive Care

> Leon S. Robertson, John Kosa,
> Margaret C. Heagarty, Robert J.
> Haggerty, and Joel J. Alpert
> Foreword by Charles A. Janeway

POVERTY, POLITICS, AND HEALTH CARE
An Appalachian Experience

> Richard A. Couto

HEALTH CARE TEAMS: An Annotated Bibliography

> Monique K. Tichy

MENTAL HEALTH AND RETARDATION POLITICS

> Dane Daniel A. Felicetti

THE PHYSICIAN'S ASSISTANT: A National and
Local Analysis

> Ann Suter Ford

HOSPITAL EFFICIENCY AND PUBLIC POLICY

> Harry I. Greenfield